Thank you purchasing,
'The Belfast Boys
and The Yangtze
Incident'.

Andy Bannister.

Contents_____

Introduction   PAGES

CHP 1 - SAMMY BANNISTER..........................8-22

CHP 2 - RAYMOND McCULLOUGH SNR..........23-26

CHP 3 - CREWMATES...................................27-31

CHP 4 - HMS AMETHYST.............................32-37

CHP 5 - THE YANGTZE INCIDENT...................38-67

CHP 6 - THE HOME COMING..........................68-83

CHP 7 - KOREAN EXPLOITS..........................84-85

CHP 8 - THE YANGTZE INCIDENT FILM.........86-92

CHP 9 - (SM) SAMMY BANNISTER.................93-106

CHP 10 - WHERE ARE THEY NOW.....…...........107-111

CHP 11 - THE GOVERNMENT ENQUIRY...........112-115

CHP 12 - THE SHIPS....................................116-119

CHP 13 - THE SHIPMATES............................120-121

CHP 14 - TWO MORE BOYS FROM BELFAST...122-126

CHP 15 - THE AMETHYST ASSOCIATION........127-129

CHP 16 - ROLL OF HONOUR..........................130-131

CHP 17 - WHAT NEXT..................................132- 137

CHP 18 – THE BELFAST BOYS
          AND THE YANGTZE INCIDENT.......138-151

(Painting by Jim Waddell)

FROM BELFAST
TO NANKING

This is the story of how some young men from both sides of the divide in Belfast and surrounding areas of Ireland, joined the ranks of the British Royal Navy. Very soon into their careers they found themselves facing the Chinese People's Liberation Army. The events took place in a war-torn China in 1949 whilst serving on board the Royal Navy Frigate, HMS Amethyst. After coming under unprovoked heavy artillery fire power, and suffering many losses, they were trapped in the jaws of their captors. Despite this, they managed a daring midnight run to freedom. Then seven decades later, two of their sons meet after a long campaign to return medals awarded to one of their fathers. They then begin to jointly campaign to have their fathers' and fellow crew mates recognized for their bravery.

(NORTHERN IRELAND BOYS) L-R   *(Pic on license from PONY5)*

McLean; **Bannister,** Murphy, **McCullough,** White, and *Haveron.*

Missing from the previous photograph of the Northern Ireland Boys, are Able Seaman, James Foster Johnston from Bangor,

Co Down and Petty Officer, John McCarthy from Larne, Co Antrim, both pictured below -original credit - The Belfast Telegraph

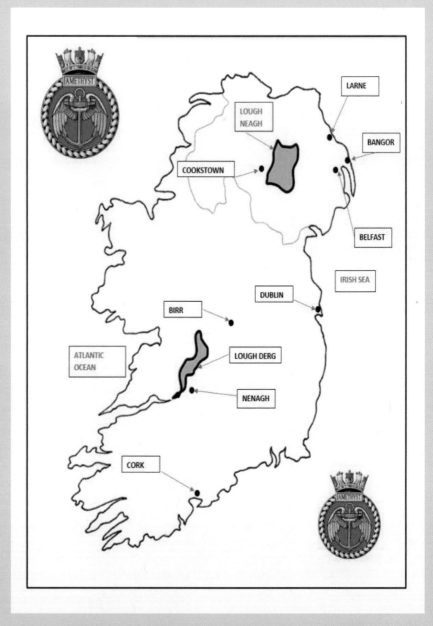

(Map of Ireland showing the homelands/cities of the fifteen Irish sailors featured in this book)

Dedicated to all those involved in the Yangtze Incident 1949

HMS Amethyst

Bannister Samuel J - Stoker Mechanic (Belfast) Wounded.

McCullough Raymond Charles Snr - Ordinary Seaman (Belfast)

McCarthy John Justin - Stores Petty Officer (Larne) MID.

McLean James - Able Seaman (Belfast)

Murphy John - Ordinary Seaman (Cookstown)

Johnston James Foster - Able Seaman (Bangor)

White Alfred - Petty Officer (Belfast)

Sinnott Patrick Joseph - Ordinary Seaman (Dublin Ireland) Killed.

Kerans John S - Lt Commander (Birr Co Offaly Ireland) DSO.

Haveron Hugh - Ordinary Seaman (Belfast)

Murphy Jerimiah - CPOSM (Timoleague, Cork Ireland)

Mullins Thomas - OS (Queenstown, Cork Ireland)

Nolan James - OS (Dublin Ireland)

(Taken from the Nominal roll of Officers; Petty Officers and seaman- HMS Amethyst – Yangtze 1949)

HMS Black Swan

McKenzie Thomas - Able Seaman (Belfast)

Burns Frederick - Able Seaman (Belfast)

HMS Black Swan

CHP1 - SAMMY BANNISTER

Schoolboy Sammy in 1939   *Stoker Sammy Bannister in 1950*

Samuel James Bannister (Sammy)

Samuel Bannister (Sammy) was born in 1928 to a working-class family and lived in the heart of Belfast City, Northern Ireland. His Rainey Street home was within touching distance of the Harland and Wolff Shipyard and at the edge of Donegall Pass, adjacent to the Ormeau Road. Belfast, at this time, had just about recovered from the blitz, and the lives lost during the First World War. People were hopeful of a new lease of life and unaware of the great depression about to hit America, with its repercussions being felt around the world. They were an exciting time with the so-called Roaring Twenties in full flow. Talking Pictures were now being shown in the cinemas and the wireless brought news to every home. Politically, 1920's Belfast was betwixt and between governments.

CHP1 - SAMMY BANNISTER

After the 1916 rising, Nationalists pushed for complete independence whilst the United Kingdom's government passed the 'Government of Ireland Act', which allowed two separate governments, one in Belfast and one in Dublin. The Dublin government was never formed and in 1929 Northern Ireland had its first all-inclusive election. All men and women over the age of 21 were entitled to vote. The Ulster Unionists gained 37 seats and the Nationalists gained 11 seats. The government at this time was based in the City Hall, Belfast until Stormont opened its doors in 1932. Industry, during this time, was mainly in the nearby shipyard, who at its peak employed over 35,000 workers. The Harland and Wolff Shipyard constructed many famous ships but is unfortunately mostly remembered for the ill-fated RMS Titanic. Many Royal Navy vessels were also constructed here, including our own HMS Belfast. HMS Belfast, now a floating museum on London's River Thames, saw a lot of action during World War Two. Launched in 1938, she went straight into action in 1939, protecting the Arctic Convoy - Russia's main supply route. Here, she engaged the German Battle cruiser, the Scharhorst, sinking her with the loss of almost its entire crew. The last ship to be constructed at Harland and Wolff was a ferry in 2003. Now the yard concentrates on engineering and ship refitting services. The Linen Mills were the next largest employer with agriculture being the third largest. Belfast's population grew enormously because of the employment opportunities. However, on a social outlook, Belfast still fell far shorter from their Great Britain counterparts, both in housing and health. 1922-24 saw Northern Ireland having the highest death rate in the United Kingdom for Tuberculosis.

CHP1 - SAMMY BANNISTER

Sammy, the second born of David and Margaret Bannister, Rainey Street Belfast, had an older sister (Lilian) and a younger brother (David Jnr). Sammy grew up to be a street wise kid, who had to learn quickly to survive in this environment. His character developed and he was soon to reach a fork in the road regarding his future, and another much more physical fork. Sammy's father, David, after serving with the Royal Artillery in Africa, returned to his Rainey Street home in Belfast, suffering the effects of Malaria. At that time, he was required to isolate himself from his family, and this isolation involved sitting on a chair at the gable wall of the end house with a heavy blanket over him for two weeks. In today's eyes this seems very primitive, but these were tough times and knowledge of fighting such diseases was not as advanced as it is today. Considering the fighting and conditions David endured before this, he was probably very glad to be sitting in this chair, in Belfast's heart. Sammy remembered being able to speak to his father at this time but having to keep his distance. Sammy would wave to his father on his way to and from school. He was very sad at night as he slept, thinking of his father having to sleep in a chair outside the family home. He worried about his dad being lonely, but his dad was a typical Belfast man. A man who feared no one; tough as nails and who had seen more than most. David was five foot six inches tall and rock solid. After doing more than his bit for his country in the First World War, David began working in a local printing firm. On Saturdays, David would sell picture frames which he had made in his spare time at the local market.

He would then take off his hat and coat to get into the boxing ring. Here, he would challenge anyone to spar with him and this was another way he brought much needed money into the Bannister home.

1939 brought the start of the Second World War and off David went again. Having fought in the First World War he was now too old to enlist but a bit of tinkering of his birth certificate saw him re-enlist with the Royall Artillery. In 1940 David was serving on the front line in Belgium. At this time Sammy was 12 years old and missed his father tremendously. Each day, on his return from school, his first question posed to his mother was, "Is there any news from dad?" The answer was invariably no. One day, when Sammy arrived home from school, he was met with what he thought to be his worst nightmare. His mother and sister were sitting at the bottom of the stairs weeping and consoling each other. Samuel's heart sank and he asked the dreaded words, "Is it my dad?" To say he was surprised at the reply is an understatement. His sister said, "No, the cat has just died." Sammy was furious that they should be so concerned about a cat and ran up the stairs shouting at them. He was so angry that he shouted, "A bloody cat, how can you cry over a bloody stupid cat!". For this, Sammy received a swift slap to the face by his mother, but he was relieved that his dad was still safe. A few weeks later two postcards arrived from the front, and they were from his father, David. The postcards brought some relief for all the family and included that Sammy, and his brother, David (Jnr) should be good boys for their mother.

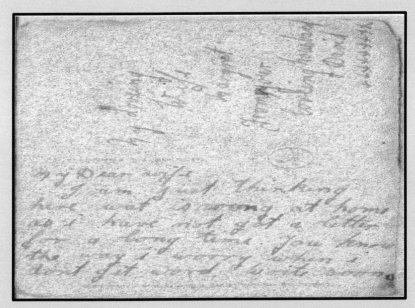

The 1st postcard reads, My Dear wife, I am just thinking here what is wrong at home as I have not got a letter for a long time. You know how I worry when I don't get word, write soon. To my loving wife Margaret from your loving husband David xxxxxxxxxx

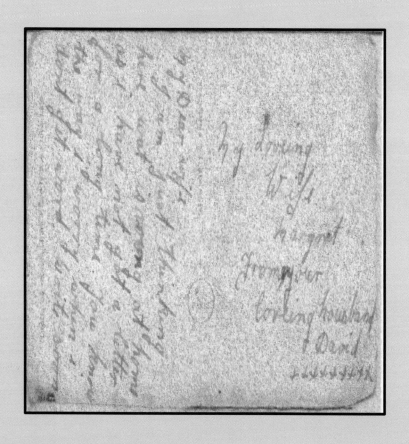

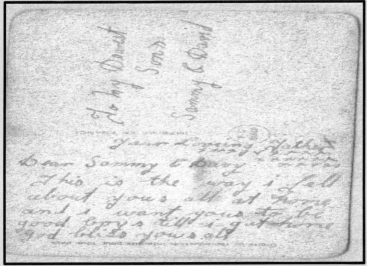

The 2nd postcard reads, Dear Sammy and Davy. This is the way I feel about you all at home *(Meaning what is written on the front of the post card)* and I want you to be good boys until I get home, God bless you all. To my Dearest sons, Sammy and Davy.

These were the last postcards received from David Bannister.

This temporary relief was short-lived as soon they were to receive the worst possible news, news they had dreaded for a long time. A telegram arrived and it was not good; unfortunately, Sammy's father, David, had been killed and was to be buried at the CWWG Dunkirk in France. This news devastated the whole family and was to have a detrimental effect on Sammy.

To this day, confusion still reigns over David's age and his exact location of falling. David had twice changed his birth certificate to fight in both the Great Wars, so his exact age is estimated. It was believed that David had fought in Dunkirk too, but the Commonwealth War Records show that he fell in Belgium.

DAVID JAMES BANNISTER KIA WW2 1940

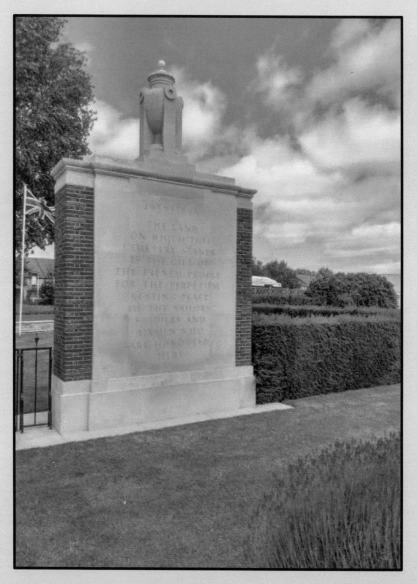

THE DUNKIRK WAR MEMORIAL CWG DUNKIRK FRANCE IN 2018

CHP 1 - SAMMY BANNISTER

This scroll commemorates

Gunner D. J. Bannister
Royal Regiment of Artillery

held in honour as one who
served King and Country in
the world war of 1939-1945
and gave his life to save
mankind from tyranny. May
his sacrifice help to bring
the peace and freedom for
which he died.

George R.I.

DAVID JAMES BANNISTER ROYAL ARTILLERY KIA 1940

CHP 1 - SAMMY BANNISTER

(Original pic courtesy of The Belfast Telegraph)

STOKER MECHANIC, SAMMY BANNISTER - ROYAL NAVY.

After his father's death, Sammy became rebellious and uninterested in schoolwork. He started running with the wrong crowd and was soon to bring trouble to the Bannister household. The police were frequent visitors and searches of the house for stolen goods was the norm. This created strife within the house, and it escalated to physical violence, which in those tough Belfast days was usually the way things were sorted out. On one occasion, as Sammy had been extremely rude to his mother and ran up the stairs, as he reached the top, he turned around and felt a sharp pain in his forehead. His mother had thrown a dinner fork at him, and it had embedded itself in his forehead. With a short tug, the fork was out and nothing more was said, both Sammy and his mother saw they had reached a point where things had escalated far enough for one day.

Unfortunately, Sammy continued in his ways and tragedy was soon to follow. After forcing entry into a local biscuit factory, his gang was being chased by the police. As they scurried along the yard walls of the backstreets, his friend fell and was impaled on a large nail, which was where the tin bathtub normally would have hung. His friend broke his neck and unfortunately died at the scene. This was a lesson Sammy never forgot and resulted in him starting to walk the straight and narrow path. Absent of a father figure, he lacked discipline and motivation. He did, however, start working for the same local printing firm his dad had worked for, mainly concerned with Hessian sack and bag printing. As days turned to weeks and weeks to years, he became disillusioned and began to create a bad time - keeping record. On one occasion, his mother was calling him to get out of his bed for work and he put one leg out of the bed to bang the floor. He shouted, "I'm up! I'm Up! Mother" but then went back to sleep. He was speedily awoken with a wet flannel on his face but to his surprise, it wasn't being placed by his mother but by his boss. Sammy's boss had had enough of his late time - keeping, so much so, that he came around to his house to sort Sammy out, once and for all. In March of 1947, when Sammy was 19, he saw an advert to join the Royal Navy. Seeing his chance to see the world and bring some stability into his life, he applied to join.

CHP 1 - SAMMY BANNISTER

His Mother thought that he just wanted to avenge his Father's death during the war and saw the Navy as his chance but at the same time she knew that military life would soon straighten him up. Sammy was accepted into the Royal Navy and was soon to be sailing the high seas. He began his basic training with HMS Excalibur. Always seeing the funny side of life, Sammy was a typical Belfast boy. There was always an opportunity for sarcasm or a joke to relieve the monotony or make light of a difficult situation. During his recruit training, Sammy was asked by the Instructing Petty Officer, "Bannister, can you swim?" to which Sammy replied, "Why, have you no ships left?" Of course, this reply wasn't warmly appreciated, and Sammy was made to do pushups until his arms could no longer hold him up. His training continued and by March 1948 he had qualified as a Stoker Mechanic serving at HMS Drake (A Royal Navy Training Establishment) until March 1949 when he received his first sea going draft. Sammy was thrilled to be joining the crew of HMS Amethyst and soon fitted into his new sea going life. He became an integral part of the Engine room staff and was excited about discovering parts of the world he had always dreamed of seeing. Life on board was tough for the junior ratings. Here, Sammy met and made many friends with his fellow shipmates and soon became a popular rating on board HMS Amethyst. On board were a few guys who were also from Northern Ireland; namely, Raymond McCullough Snr; James McClean, Johnny Murphy, John McCarthy, James Foster Johnston, Alfred White, and Hugh Haveron, pictured on page three.

CHP 1 - SAMMY BANNISTER

HMS Amethyst (pic courtesy of David Page Navyphotos.uk)

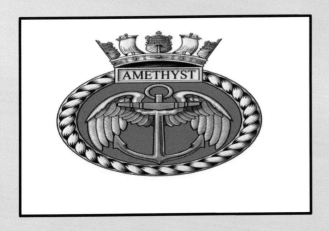

CHP 2 - RAYMOND McCULLOUGH (SNR)

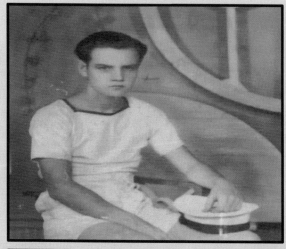

Age 16

Age 19

Boy Seaman, Raymond McCullough Snr, on board Amethyst in Hong Kong, 1949.

(Pics courtesy of Raymond McCullough Jnr)

CHP 2 - RAYMOND McCULLOUGH (SNR)

Raymond McCullough Senior was born in 1930. He was the eldest son of Mr. and Mrs. McCullough late of Islandbawn Drive, Belfast. He had two brothers and three sisters. Raymond Senior grew up in Belfast and during the 2nd World War, he, along with his siblings, was evacuated to the coastal town of Ardglass, Co Down. Fortunately for them, the evacuation wasn't to some stranger's house but the home of their Grandparents, Jimmy and Cathleen Smith. Jimmy and Cathleen lived in a small group of terraced houses between Hill Street and Kildare Street facing the sea. Together with their cousins, Alec and Terry, they enjoyed all things coastal and anything to do with the sea. This move was an adventure for them all and much removed from the busy city life back in Belfast. The threat of the German bombers was much less here and in turn life was more relaxed. Raymond Snr enjoyed his time there immensely, fishing, exploring, and enjoying the comings and goings of a busy fishing port. He spent days out on the boats catching mackerel and cod to bring back to his Grandparents. Like many a boy, the mystery of the sea was eventually to draw him towards a life on the ocean wave. As the Second World War continued, he returned to his native Belfast home and like everyone else, tried to get on with normal life, as far as he could. Raymond Senior left primary school in 1942 and attended the Christian Brother's College on Belfast's Crumlin Road. Here, he studied ten different subjects in preparation for his Junior Certificate Exam. At the age of fifteen he left the College to begin work in Mackey's, a local engineering firm. Here, he worked in the drawing office as a Junior Clerk, where all the plans were drawn up for the staff.

CHP 2 - RAYMOND McCULLOUGH (SNR)

It's believed that Raymond Snr, also enlisted in Naval Cadet training at the age of fifteen and a half, having assured the Training Staff he was a year older. Then, in 1946, he advanced to the ranks of the Royal Navy as a Boy Class Two Rating. Although he enjoyed working at Mackey's, the sea was calling him so loudly that he had to follow his dreams. As his training continued, he was soon a Boy First Class Rating. He then joined the ranks on board HMS Amethyst in 1948 as a fully qualified Ordinary Seaman, where he was to spend the next year and eight months.

Film Star looks from Raymond McCullough Snr.

(Pic courtesy of Raymond McCullough Jnr)

Not all sea life is plain sailing-Secure it or lose it.

(Pic Courtesy of Raymond McCullough Jnr)

CHP 3 - HMS AMETHYST CREWMATES

Johnny Murphy

Able Seaman, Johnny Murphy.

(Pic courtesy of Ciaran Murphy)

Johnny Murphy was born in 1929 and grew up in Cookstown, Co Tyrone Northern Ireland. He had five brothers and two sisters. Cookstown lies to the west of Lough Neagh and is approximately forty miles from Belfast. Johnny enjoyed all things rural and experienced a much more pleasant and relaxed upbringing being away from the dog-eat-dog atmosphere of Belfast. Johnny also lost his father at a young age. His father was a soldier, Pte John Joseph Murphy, in the Pioneer Corp, on board RMS Lancastria, an ocean liner requisitioned by the UK Government. She was sunk in 1940 during Operation Aerial. An operation to evacuate British Troops and civilians but she was sunk with the loss of thousands of lives. So, both Sammy Bannister and Johnny Murphy's fathers are buried in the Commonwealth War Graves in Dunkirk Cemetery, France.

CHP 3 - HMS AMETHYST CREWMATES

Johnny Murphy

When Johnny left school, he began his working life as a Trainee Plasterer but soon into his training a severe winter hit the country and most, if not all building work was suspended. So, as he approached the winter of 1947, and the fear of no work being available, Johnny enlisted in the Royal Navy. He began his naval career as an Ordinary Seaman. In January 1949 he was drafted to HMS Amethyst and soon teamed up with the Northern Ireland boys on board. Johnny advanced to Able Seaman and was trained to operate all the ships weaponry.

Johnny Murphy with a shipmate. (Pic courtesy of Ciaran Murphy)

James Foster Johnston

(Original pic courtesy of The Belfast Telegraph)

James was from the seaside town of Bangor, Co Down, so sea life was a natural progression for him.

John McCarthy (Petty Officer)

(Original pic courtesy of The Belfast Telegraph)

John came from the busy Larne Harbour area, Co Antrim and saw the Royal Navy as his natural progression to a life on the ocean wave.

CHP 3 - HMS AMETHYST CREWMATES

(Pic on license from PONY5)

Seaman, James

McClean, Petty Officer, Alfred White, and Seaman, Hugh Haveron all Belfast men. It was a clear choice of working on the ships in the nearby shipyard or a life of sailing the seas.

Boy Seaman, Patrick Joseph Sinnott.

From Nenagh, Co Tipperary Ireland.

Not too much is known about Patrick. He came from Nenagh, Co Tipperary, Ireland and lived near Lough Derg, one of Ireland's largest inland lakes. Lough Derg has always been popular for boating and sailing but can be treacherous in bad weather. Nenagh is close to Limerick where the River Shannon meets the Atlantic Ocean.

(Pic Courtesy of Raymond McCullough Jnr)

A model of HMS Amethyst made by Raymond McCullough Jnr-
with HMS Caroline in the Background.

(Pic courtesy of Paul McErlane)

CHP 4 - HMS AMETHYST

HMS Amethyst was a Sloop Black Swan class ship, reclassified as a Frigate in 1947. She was constructed in 1943 by Alexander and Stephen and Sons Ltd of Glasgow, Scotland. Launched in May 1943, she saw numerous battles and played her part in the Korean War of 1950-1953; Amethyst continued in active service until 1957.

(Picture courtesy of David Page-Navyphotos.uk)

(HMS Amethyst)

CHP 4 - HMS AMETHYST

In 1949 she had a ship's company of one hundred and eighty men, one dog and one cat. The junior ratings mess deck was furnished with hammocks, which were slung to the side to allow for daily living quarters (Mess Deck). Life on board was busy, with each man assigned his daily work routine as well as taking their turn for watch duties, being that at night or during the day.

See example of a sea going watch system below.

NAME	TIME
FIRST WATCH	20.00-00.00
MIDDLE WATCH	00.00-04.00
MORNING WATCH	04.00-08.00
FORENOON WATCH	08.00-12.00
AFTERNOON WATCH	12.00-16.00
FIRST DOG WATCH	16.00-18.00
SECOND DOG WATCH	18.00-20.00

All ships, and Amethyst was no different, fought a never-ending battle against the sea and weather conditions. Constant ship's husbandry took place each day with everyone playing their part. From cleaning to maintenance and everything in-between. This is where the old seaman adage, *'If it doesn't move, paint it'*, comes from. So constant painting took place to minimize corrosion and prolong the life of the ship.

Ship's husbandry on board HMS Amethyst during her far eastern exploits.

(Pic courtesy of Raymond McCullough Jnr)

It would be unheard of today to have a dog or cat on board a Royal Navy vessel but Petty Officer Griffiths, who was the cook on board Amethyst, managed to get his trusted dog Peggy on the ship. I would imagine Peggy was well fed on scraps but found living on ships to be a struggle. However, it was a different story for the adopted ship's cat, Simon. He made Amethyst his home during a port visit to Hong Kong in January 1948. The cat became very important to the crew, especially when they were docked at port.

CHP 4 - HMS AMETHYST

This is when ships or indeed any boat is most vulnerable to pests. The main offenders were rats, who would make their way along the ropes (Mooring Lines) used to secure the ship to the dock. At night they would also sneak along the gangway. Once on board, there were so many places for them to hide and if not detected they would cause chaos once at sea. Therefore, a good cat was a vital piece of equipment in those days. The Navy also used an ingenious piece of kit, in their fight against these pests. They placed 'Rodent Discs' along the securing ropes to stop the rats being able to get on board.

(Picture courtesy of David Page-Navyphotos.uk)

(Rodent discs on Amethyst's mooring lines)

CHP 4 - HMS AMETHYST

The average age of the men on board Amethyst was twenty-four, which seems extremely young to be in such important roles. For many of the younger ratings, this was their first sea going experience and they had to learn quickly. Some struggled with the rough seas, and some struggled with living in such small confines, with little privacy or places to go on the ship for some solace. Arguments or disputes were frequent amongst the ratings which was no surprise. However, this would all change very soon as an instruction coming from the Admiralty would gel everyone together.

(Photos courtesy of R McCullough Jnr)

Peggy - on board HMS Amethyst

& Simon - *HMS Amethyst's rat catcher*

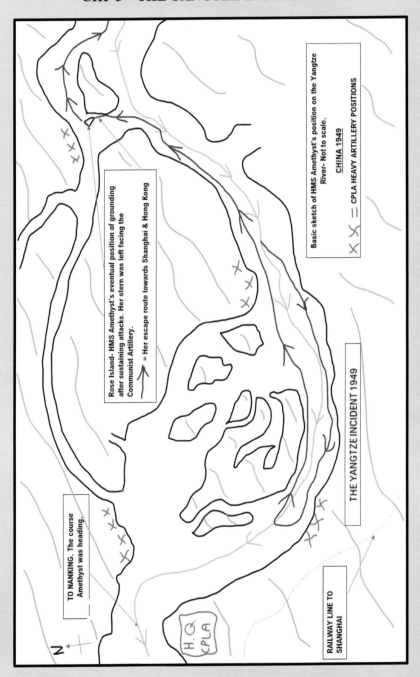

Rose Island- HMS Amethyst's eventual position of grounding after sustaining attacks. Her stern was left facing the Communist Artillery.

↑ = Her escape route towards Shanghai & Hong Kong

Basic sketch of HMS Amethyst's position on the Yangtze River- Not to scale.

CHINA 1949

X X = CPLA HEAVY ARTILLERY POSITIONS

THE YANGTZE INCIDENT 1949

TO NANKING. The course Amethyst was heading.

H.Q. CPLA

RAILWAY LINE TO SHANGHAI

N

The Yangtze River.

The Yangtze River is the longest river in China and Asia. Running from its source in Tibet, it stretches over 3900 miles to the East China Sea. It has always been the most important river in China with a third of the population sharing its banks. Being the main export/import route, the locals call it Ghang Jiang (Long River) or Da Jiang (Great River).

HMS AMETHYST. *(Courtesy of David Page-Navyphotos.uk)*

CHP 5 - THE YANGTZE INCIDENT 1949

In early April 1949, orders came from the Admiralty in London that HMS Amethyst was to make her way to Nanking, China with supplies for and to relieve, HMS Consort. Amethyst was part of the 'Far East Fleet', on constant patrol of the far eastern waters. Consort was a guard ship for British subjects and was moored in Nanking. China, at this time, was teetering towards a possible end of its civil war. A war between Mao Tse-tung's Communist Army and Chiang Kai-Shek's Nationalist Army. Royal Navy ships were supposedly free to use Chinese waters since the 1858 'Treaty of Tiensin' but were always aware of imminent danger. The danger was that the Nationalists reluctantly honoured the treaty, and the Communists didn't. So, on the 19th of April 1949 HMS Amethyst slipped from Shanghai making her way along the Yangtze River in China, towards Nanking. After eight hours approximately of sailing she anchored at Kuang Yin on the Yangtze River. Here she made fast until first light the following morning. On the 20th of April 1949 HMS Amethyst, with the Northern Ireland boys on board, left Kuang Yin and made for Nanking. Amethyst stopped briefly due to poor visibility, then continued on her way. As she steamed along the river, small arms fire was sustained from the banks of the Yangtze. "Action Stations" were called, and all crew responded as per training drills. The exact location of the enemy could not be ascertained so return fire was not engaged. Amethyst steamed on but was then attacked by heavy artillery, this time causing serious casualties and killing some sailors outright. One of the injured was Stoker Sammy Bannister. He was blown off his feet along with two of his shipmates.

CHP 5 - THE YANGTZE INCIDENT 1949

When he came to, he felt a severe burning in his chest. He had been hit with a piece of shrapnel which had embedded itself deep in his chest and he was struggling for breath. As he was helped to his feet by SM Maddocks, he noticed another shipmate who was in much more trouble than him; this poor guy had lost half his face in the attack and was in a fight for his life. Fellow sailors came to their aid and rushed them to the mess deck for treatment. OS Raymond McCullough Snr was one of those sailors who administered first aid and risked his own skin to ensure others got the treatment they needed. The next attack on Amethyst resulted in the voice pipe and power switchboards being disabled. The damage sustained meant only certain guns could return fire and communication to the engine room was extremely difficult. Soon Amethyst was to run aground on one of the Yangtze's many sandbanks. This sandbank was adjacent to Rose Island and Amethyst was cruelly positioned with her stern facing direct fire. It was on her stern that she sustained a massive piercing hole by heavy artillery. Lt Weston assumed command even though he was injured, and he issued an order to take all wounded ashore. During this time Amethyst was still under heavy gunfire and many of the injured were killed whilst trying to disembark. The order for abandon ship was made and all those who could move were to try and abandon ship. Many of the wounded were still being treated in the mess deck and could not get off the ship. Around sixty ratings who had made it into the water were fired upon and the order was given for no more men to leave the ship. Confusion reigned, and it took time to ascertain who had left the ship.

Of those who made it ashore, some eventually made their way to Shanghai; others were killed, and some returned to the ship. Once onto the shore, Stoker Sammy Bannister struggled for breath and a fellow shipmate, Boy Keith Martin, was limping. They were both easily taken by the CPLA (Chinese People's Liberation Army) who took them to a village hospital. When they arrived at the village hospital, Sammy was made aware that he needed an operation but being a village hospital, they had no access to anesthetic or pain relief. Sammy told them to go ahead and operate as he knew it was his only chance of survival. As he lay on the operating table, he was given a rag to bite on for the pain. The village doctor successfully removed the shrapnel from Sammy's chest, to his, and everyone else's relief. Boy Martin had his ankle treated and bandaged as both sailors came to realize that they were now being held as hostages.

(Pic-Author's copy)

(Major damage inflicted on Amethyst during the attack)

(Small and heavy arms damage to Amethyst's bridge and wheelhouse)

(Pics courtesy of David Smith)

CHP 5 - THE YANGTZE INCIDENT 1949

Amethyst got word to HMS Consort who made way to come to her rescue. It was thought Consort could possibly tow Amethyst free from the sandbank she was stuck on. Preparation for this took place whilst casualties were being tended to. A white flag was hoisted to accompany the Union Jacks already displayed but still the small arms fire came from the banks towards Amethyst. This hampered the rescue of the gunners and those casualties exposed on the upper decks. Consort came soon after and found it impossible to get near Amethyst to help. HMS Consort came under heavy fire but was able to return fire, only to pass Amethyst and get to a safer area down river. More unsuccessful attempts to help Amethyst were made soon after, by HMS London and HMS Black Swann. They too received heavy fire from the CPLA guns and sustained damage and casualties, although they tried bravely to free Amethyst, they could not sustain anymore from the communist arsenal and had to retreat. In the dead of night, Amethyst tried to free herself but although she freed herself from the bank, she came under small arms fire again and anchored up stream. A CPLA Officer arrived on board offering Sampans to evacuate the wounded. An RAF Sunderland Flying boat landed and a doctor made it on board Amethyst, but the Sunderland had to take off again as she came under fire. On the 22nd of April 1949 all casualties were successfully off loaded but Captain Skinner died of his wounds. Later that day, Amethyst moved approximately ten miles but was attacked again even though she had her Union Jacks unfurled. She dropped anchor and the order was given that seventeen of the dead were to be prepared for burial.

At this, the Sunderland arrived again carrying Lt Cdr JS Kerans, he had been stationed at Nanking, and was now in charge of Amethyst. An order to try and escape to Nanking was quashed by Naval Authorities at Hong Kong; instead, an order was given to be prepared to have to destroy ship. All confidential documents and orders were destroyed in preparation. Temporary repairs to keep Amethyst watertight took place during the next few days and normal shipping traffic was starting to resume use of the Yangtze River.

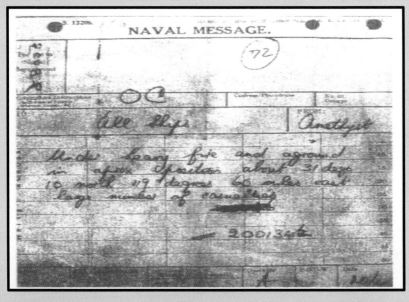

Message reads - Under heavy fire and aground, approx. position about 31 degrees 10' north, 119 degrees 60' East. Large number of casualties.

(Author's copy of original message, telling Amethyst's position and current state)

CHP 5 - THE YANGTZE INCIDENT 1949

A delegation from Amethyst was summoned to the shore for negotiations. The delegation met with the Artillery Commander who had opened fire. Amethyst was told that the Chinese believed that Amethyst opened fire first, but if she remained where she was, there would be no further artillery fire sustained. These meetings continued and LT KS Hett, representing the Navy at these meetings, was met with the same ideology from the Artillery Commander that Amethyst opened fire first. Lt Hett enquired about the missing ratings, Stoker Mechanic Sammy Bannister, and Boy Seaman Keith Martin, but there was no news on their whereabouts. A meeting with the CPLA Colonel Kang was requested by Lt Hett but was not guaranteed.

At this time, telegrams were being sent to all back home to inform them of their loved ones. For Bannister and Martin this realization of their status as hostages became more real as the days went on. The Colonel of the CPLA, Col Kang visited them many times and insisted they gave signed statements to him. He wanted Stoker Sammy Bannister and Boy Seaman Keith Martin to say that HMS Amethyst fired on the CPLA first and both sailors refused to give such statements. Even being two young men, not knowing what they would face next, they held their nerve. Many days of negotiations between the CPLA and HMS Amethyst Senior Ranks for the two sailors' release dragged on. Eventually, Boy Martin snapped and said he would give a statement. Sammy was outraged and suggested to Boy Martin that he keep his mouth shut.

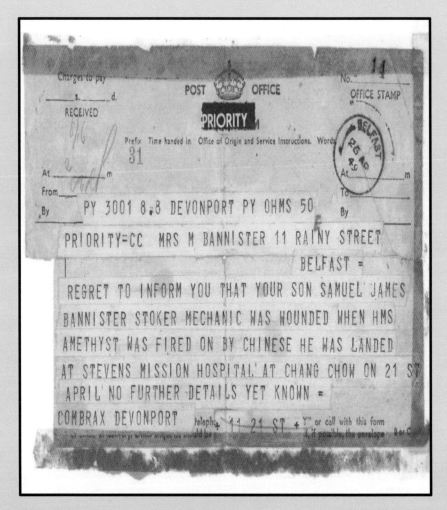

(Worrying news for the Bannister household back in Belfast – but nonetheless relieved that Sammy was still alive)

Boy Martin insisted but when it came to giving his statement, he would not allow his captors to put words in his mouth. Instead, he told the Colonel of the CPLA that it was them, the CPLA, who fired first and attacked HMS Amethyst. The CPLA Colonel was not best pleased with this statement and so Sammy and Boy Martin were held captive for much longer. Negotiations continued for the release of the two sailors who were now beginning to despair. The CPLA knew Amethyst was on a sandbank and going nowhere; they also knew that Sammy and Boy Martin were never going to give false statements, so it was futile to continue their capture. Lt Hett was made aware that he had to deliver a formal request for the two sailors' release, which he did immediately. On Wed 25th May 1949 a message came through that Bannister and Martin were onshore awaiting safe return to Amethyst. Lt Hett went ashore and brought both ratings safely back onboard. Stoker Mechanic Bannister and Boy Seaman Martin stated that they had been treated well. Upon interview it came to light that both men were treated for their respective injuries, but Bannister was still poorly after his operation. He recounted how the hospital had no anesthetic, so he had told them to operate on him without it. He confirmed that they removed shrapnel from his chest which was affecting his breathing, whilst he bit down hard on a gauze type cloth. Although primitive, the hospital had indeed saved his life. The ratings then told of how they were frightened and put under pressure to make statements. They reported how they were asked to say that Amethyst opened fire first and caused the retaliation. Neither rating would agree or sign such documents to the frustration of Col Kang and the CPLA.

Even the sustained pressure and the thought of never getting back to Amethyst, never mind home, wasn't enough to break them. They knew the implications of any false statements would endanger their colleagues and indeed their country. Both Bannister and Martin were assigned light duties and given time to recover from their ordeal. They were overjoyed to be reunited with their shipmates and tried to settle into their new norm. Many fellow shipmates wanted to know their story and rallied round to support them. Stoker Bannister still found breathing difficult due to the humidity and both ratings were reluctant to spend too much time on the upper decks, for fear of another CPLA attack.

Stoker Sammy Bannister   *Boy Seaman Keith Martin*

(Pics - Authors copies)

CHP 5 - THE YANGTZE INCIDENT 1949

Able Seaman Johnny Murphy (Pic courtesy of Ciaran Murphy)

A/Seaman Raymond McCullough Snr

(Pic courtesy of Raymond McCullough Jnr)

On board Amethyst a head count was taking place. Every man had to be accounted for and up to date communication made to the Naval Command in Nanking and back home. Shanghai also played their part in this census. This was welcome news for the McCullough family back in Belfast. It was initially thought that OS Raymond McCullough Snr had left Amethyst and not returned but he had returned to the ship and was still active in tending to the injured onboard. This confirmation was sent to the McCullough household.

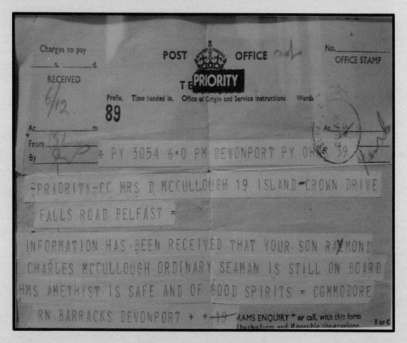

(Welcome news to the McCullough family household. Pic courtesy of Raymond McCullough Jnr)

CHP 5 - THE YANGTZE INCIDENT 1949

Life on board Amethyst was getting tougher. Steam: electricity and rations were now in short supply. Water was being rationed for washing and drinking. About a month in from initial grounding, despondency was beginning to creep in, and morale was low. Several meetings between Lt Cdr Kerans and Col Kang took place over the next few weeks but remained fruitless. The humdrum days became weeks, and the highlight was the news that mail was on its way from Shanghai, but it was up to the CPLA if it could be delivered to Amethyst. Lt Cdr Kerans sent a message to the Admiralty to say how no commanding officer could ask for a better group of men, he was so encouraged by their resolve and teamwork. On Sun 12th June 1949 a delegation from Amethyst went ashore at Col Kang's request. Amongst the members of the delegation was PO McCarthy from Larne in N Ireland. At this meeting Col Kang insisted he would allow Amethyst back down the river if he was given the order by his superiors in Nanking. Col Kang was feeling the pressure now. He had to resolve this issue and insisted he was being as helpful as he could to all who were suffering onboard Amethyst. The heat and general health issues were now influencing all those onboard, so the crew were very grateful to the RAF Doctor Fl Lt Fearnley attending to them. Good news came from the latest meeting between Lt Cdr Kerans and Col Kang, the mail was going to be allowed to be brought to Amethyst. This greatly improved morale for all those onboard but like a double-edged sword, Col Kang insisted that replenishment of Amethyst by a merchant ship would never be allowed to take place. However, if he received a written statement that the British warship fired first, then he would allow Amethyst safe passage down the river.

CHP 5 - THE YANGTZE INCIDENT 1949

The mail arrived as promised on Fri 24th June 1949. Many onboard read and re-read their mail as it had been more than seventy days since any mail being received. On the 30th of June 1949 Amethyst was allowed to receive an oil delivery from Nanking but nothing else. The crew were informed that the CPLA would be having a week of parades and celebrations, so no meetings would be held with them during this incoming week. A BBC broadcast of tunes brought some relief to the crew. It was a mixture of tunes played on Listeners Choice for the crew of HMS Amethyst. On the 5th of July 1949 a meeting took place with Lt Cdr Kerans and Col Kang. It was reported back that Kerans was a true diplomat and handled every meeting, including this one, with the utmost professionalism. Col Kang stated that the General was not happy that the British had not admitted to invading Chinese waters. He also did not think that Lt Cdr Kerans was authorized to represent the Admiral of the British Navy. Lt Cdr Kerans assured Col Kang that he was authorized and always had been. Col Kang insisted he needed written acknowledgement from the Admiral that the British Warships invaded the Chinese waters. Lt Cdr Kerans assured Col Kang that he would not use the word 'invade' as this meant intent. He further explained that at no stage was there intention to invade China or Chinese waters because British warships were neutral and passed through these waters as neutral visitors. Lt Cdr Kerans told Col Kang that it was a fault of the ship's aide that they had entered the CPLA zone of the river, and not an intentional act of defiance; the word invade would never be used in any British letter to the General as Britain was a friendly nation towards China.

CHP 5 - THE YANGTZE INCIDENT 1949

Much toing and froing regarding translation prolonged the meeting but Lt Cdr Kerans insisted his handwritten letter regarding HMS Amethyst's intentions was sufficient to allow Amethyst safe passage and should appease the General. Lt Cdr Kerans requested that his pilotage charts were returned to him for safe passage back down the Yangtze River. Col Kang informed Lt Cdr Kerans that a pilot would be supplied to help him down river. The two men discussed the safe pilotage arrangements and agreed to meet again. To lighten the mood, Lt Cdr Kerans asked if the Col could put an end to the incessant rain? - No response was given, probably lost in translation or a lack of military sense of humour. The much-needed oil arrived from Nanking, delayed due to bad weather rather than Chinese interference. Everyone on board was delighted and even looked forward to the hard slog of getting the barrels of oil on board. The whole crew worked solidly to bring on the two hundred and ninety-six drums of oil. It took them eleven hours of non-stop graft to complete this, much to the captain's delight. No one had trouble sleeping that night, but those of the crew who were on watch duty, had extra rations of coffee to help them stay alert.

CHP 5 - THE YANGTZE INCIDENT 1949

(Pic courtesy of Raymond McCullough Jnr)

Spirits remained high due to the captain being summoned to a meeting with the CPLA in Chaing Kiang on the 11th of July 1949. Usually this meant that the General of the CPLA would be in attendance and progress might be made. Unfortunately, this was not the case, the General was not in attendance at the meeting and Col Kang was his usual belligerent self. The captain returned from the meeting very disconsolate due to Col Kang informing him that rations would no longer be provided for the crew of HMS Amethyst. The crew were going to have to live on half rations which was another form of getting the captain to give in and sign a letter to say that Amethyst fired first. The crew were as determined not to give in as the captain was. The captain also was informed by Col Kang that no supply boat or ship would be allowed to come aside Amethyst to sell goods; if they did, they would be destroyed, and Amethyst would be destroyed if she tried to move position at all.

The captain had a memo to all on board typed up and placed for the crew to read. It was basically to say that 'loose lips sink ships', and that no one was to talk in the presence of any Chinese interpreters or Chinese visitors, as this could compromise the whole ship. He also posted on the noticeboard a letter from the Commander in Chief of the Navy which gave the whole ship's company a much-needed morale boost. To further boost morale, the captain insisted on having group photos taken on deck to show the CPLA on shore that the crew were in good spirits.

(Pic courtesy of Mick Hickinbottom, proud son of George Hickinbottom)

(Bannister, McCullough, and Murphy – circled)

Stoker Bannister was still recovering from his ordeal and Johnny Murphy still sported a bruise to his head, resulting from a shell casing which had caught him off guard.

Much needed supplies being delivered to HMS Amethyst by sampan.

(Pic courtesy of Gilly O'Reilly - proud daughter of Stewart Hett)

CHP 5 - THE YANGTZE INCIDENT 1949

The crew of HMS Amethyst experienced the hottest day so far on the 20th of July 1949. The heat was unbearable, and the fans were blowing hot air. No one could sleep and everyone was wringing wet with perspiration. On the 22nd of July 1949 the captain was once again summoned to a meeting with the CPLA. Hopes were high for this meeting as it had been ten days since the last meeting. The captain returned with bad news, the CPLA still wanted a letter from the Admiral of the Fleet before they would consider Amethyst's position. The General of the CPLA would still not recognize Lt Cdr Kerans as the Admiral's representative until he got a signed letter. The General and Col Kang were under pressure and scrutiny from the Chinese and in turn made the crew of Amethyst live a life of hell in the heat with little cool air or provisions. The Col said he would try and get the crew some more oil and provisions through from Nanking. As some light relief, the captain had brought back four bottles of beer which were balloted off for each mess; the lucky winners were delighted as it had been over three months from they tasted a beer. Due to the heat the mosquitos and rats became a worse problem than usual. Amethyst was a sitting target in many senses and the ship's cat Simon, had his work cut out with the rats. But soon another pest was on its way. Typhoon Gloria was forecast to be passing over and all makeshift awnings were removed in preparation for her arrival. On Mon 25th July 1949 in she came, and the Yangtze River was the roughest anyone had witnessed in the whole time they had been there. The second anchor was dropped to keep Amethyst steady.

CHP 5 - THE YANGTZE INCIDENT 1949

If the chain had broken with the strain, Amethyst might have moved and then the CPLA would have opened up on her, so tensions were high, both on the chains and the crew. Typhoon Gloria came and went just as quickly. The anchors held and afterwards the Yangtze started showing signs that the storm had blown over. The debris started floating by Amethyst and much to everyone's amusement a few hay bales passed with a poor dog riding along on the top of it. Following soon after was a pig swimming by and some of the crew did their utmost to lasso the pig. A second pig also came swimming by, and again vain attempts were made to lasso it. The crew were so disappointed as they had envisaged a roast pork barbeque. On Sat 30th July 1949, one hundred and two days after being grounded, the captain called a meeting with some senior ranks. At this meeting he informed them that he had made a decision about Amethyst and her plight. The captain (Lt Cdr Kerans) explained what was to happen. All the crew were informed and slowly and quietly they went about their orders, so as not to attract any unwelcome reaction from the CPLA, on the banks of the Yangtze. On Sunday 31st July 1949, the captain's orders had been carried out. Amethyst had greased her anchor chains, changed her silhouette by way of tarpaulins and everyone was ready. Most ships carried canvas tarpaulins to use as awnings in extreme heat, thus keeping the heat from penetrating the decks and from igniting the explosives kept on board. Under the cover of darkness, the order went out to slip anchors and away she floated. Engines engaged and she was off. Lt Hett navigated the many sandbanks and orders were barked back and forth.

Amethyst listed from side to side and at one stage ploughed through a Chinese Junk. The CPLA saw that their sitting target was now a moving target; they immediately fired on Amethyst, but she made good ground. At the same time, a Chinese passenger ship came past Amethyst in the opposite direction. This passenger ship took direct hits which had been aimed at Amethyst. As Amethyst bravely fought her way through the CPLA attacks and the treacherous sandbanks, word came through that HMS Concord was in sight. Amethyst had done it! The captain sent a signal which became the most famous signal ever made by a British warship,

```
NRX6/ 926/ 30

    EMERGENCY

    FROM        H M S AMETHYST        3020322

    TO          C IN C FES

    INOF        ADMTY

                A C N B

                FAR EAST STATION

    BT

    HAVE REJOINED THE FLEET SOUTH OF WOOSUNG.

    NO DAMAGE OR CASUALTIES.

    OOD SAVE THE KING.

    BT ..... 3020322

    .+.+.+.
```

The Commander-in-Chief of the Far East Station, Admiral Sir Patrick Brind, replied as below.

The Commander-in-Chief of the Far East Station, Admiral Sir Patrick Brind, replied as below.

THE COMMANDER IN CHIEF FAR EAST STATION REPLIED AS FOLLOWS.

WELCOME BACK TO THE FLEET. WE ARE ALL EXTREMELY PROUD OF YOURMOST

GALLANT AND SKILLFUL ESCAPE AND THAT THE ENDURANCE AND FORTITUDE

DISPLAYED BY EVERYONE HAS BEEN REWARDED WITH SUCH SUCCESS.

YOUR BEARING IN ADVERSITY AND YOUR DARING PASSAGE TONIGHT WILL

BE EPIC IN THE HISTORY OF THE NAVY ENDS

Now telegrams were being sent to all families back home, this one was sent to Mrs. Augustyns, mother of Petty Officer Denis Augustyns.

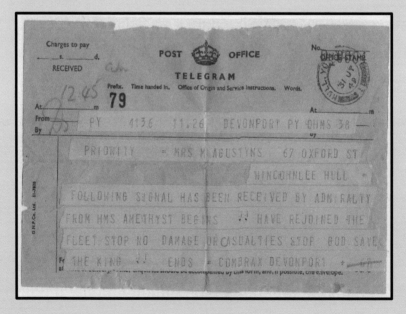

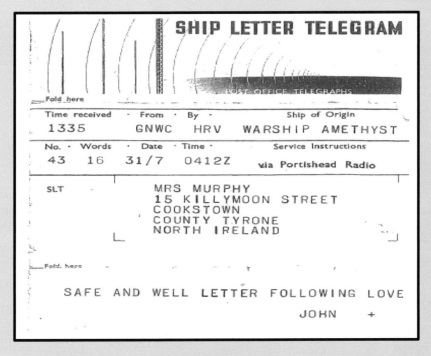

Welcome news for the Murphy family back in Cookstown,

Northern Ireland.

(Pic courtesy of Ciaran Murphy)

Once Amethyst reached HMS Concord, they both moved to a safe area. Here the jubilation was muted as a job still had to be done. Amethyst needed more oil and temporary repairs to make her seaworthy. Some of Concord's crew transferred onto HMS Amethyst to assist with manning her until they met up with the crew who had escaped to Shanghai. Her orders were to make her way to Hong Kong where she would be met by some of the fleet and fully repaired. She had done it, the most daring escape to victory a British warship has ever achieved.

CHP 5 - THE YANGTZE INCIDENT 1949

Her crew were ecstatic to be free, thoughts of seeing family, drinking infinite amounts of water (and other liquids) and being clean and tidy were rushing through their heads. Sadness, for the lives lost and wounded sailors, was very apparent as they were now free (literally) to express their emotions. Survivors guilt was sweeping through the ship, but these guys were made of stern stuff, and they pushed on through the torment. HMS Jamaica was waiting for Amethyst to accompany her to Hong Kong; she had mail and rations for all the crew of Amethyst. Their months of hell on the Yangtze River were over.

HM King George VI

The king sent his personal signal to HMS Amethyst

"Please convey to the Commanding Officer and ship's company of HMS Amethyst my hearty congratulations on their daring exploit to rejoin the Fleet. The courage, skill and determination shown by all on board have my highest commendation. Splice the mainbrace."
George R

Splice the mainbrace is a navy term for a celebratory ration of rum, originally it was a term used for everyone needing a stiff drink after completing one of the most dangerous repair jobs on a sailing ship.

H.M.S
AMETHYST
1949

HMS Amethyst limping into Hong Kong.

(Pic courtesy of David Bannister, proud son of Stoker Sammy Bannister)

As the British Cruiser Jamaica circled Amethyst north of Formosa, the Second in command of the Far East Station, Admiral Madden, sent a message to the crew of Amethyst. *"I am most proud that my Flagship shares the honour of escorting your valiant ship to Hong Kong where the Commander-In-Chief is waiting to welcome you back to his fleet"* to which Amethyst replied, *"It is a great moment".*

CHP 5 - THE YANGTZE INCIDENT 1949

The crew of HMS Jamaica salute HMS Amethyst as she rejoins the fleet.

(Pics courtesy of Ray Augustyns, proud son of PO Denis Augustyns)

Jubilant Welcome British sailors (foreground) jubilantly salute the sloop Amethyst off North Formosa after the ship's daring escape from Chinese Communist captivity in the Yangtze River. The sloop had been trapped in the river since April 20 when it was beached during a duel with Red artillery.

(A battered but not defeated HMS Amethyst entering Hong Kong, her wounds clearly visible)

(Pic now in the public domain, original pic credited to Frank Goldsworthy)

In Hong Kong, Amethyst received much needed repairs and a fresh lick of paint. The ordeal for the crew may have been over but the weather, as usual, played a significant role in what happened to Amethyst. The night before she was due to set off for England, another typhoon hit the shores of Hong Kong, according to the South China Morning Post Newspaper.

CHP 5 - THE YANGTZE INCIDENT 1949

Its journalist, Frank Goldsworthy reported that one hundred mile an hour gusts had wreaked havoc in the region. Commercial airlines were warned to stay away and those planes which were on the nearby airfield were severely damaged. Many Chinese ships were pushed aground and some perished. A horrific night was had by all and the men on Amethyst must have thought they would never see home.

(Pic courtesy of G Hikkinbottom)

(A much happier Kerans leaving Hong Kong)

CHP 6 - THE HOME COMING

Leaving Hong Kong for the long journey home, HMS Amethyst repaired and repainted but with men on board still wounded both mentally and physically.

(Pic courtesy of Reuters UK)

Many of the crew, including Stoker Bannister, were mightily relieved to be returning home. Nearing exhaustion, together with the horrors of this experience, was showing on everyone's faces. The horizon was a glimpse of hope and a goal to achieve. The crew were in mourning but remained professional in all that they did.

CHP 6 - THE HOME COMING

There was no time for feeling sorry for oneself and being at sea ensured that the normality of sea life would help take the crew's mind off their past ordeal. Routine tasks and duties made them feel almost normal again, but it was just putting off the inevitable. Each crew member had to decompartmentalize and ensure the mental and physical scars did not affect their reliability to one another. The long journey home began with a first port of call in Singapore. Later, they were to visit Penang, Colombo, Aden, Port Said, Malta, Gibraltar and then Plymouth, England.

HMS Amethyst in dry dock, Malta, fully covered in canvas due to the extreme heat.

(Pic courtesy of Reuters UK)

CHP 6 - THE HOME COMING

A scheduled stop in Malta allowed the crew some much needed R&R with many trying to stay cool, and deal with the aftermath of their ordeal. HMS Amethyst had her hull anti-fouled and repainted here.

(Pics courtesy of Raymond McCullough Jnr)

CHP 6 - THE HOME COMING

Stoker Bannister takes time out to send his mother a post card from Malta and it's clear the water rationing during the Yangtze Incident is still affecting him.

The card reads - Dear Mother.....I hope this card finds you and all at home in the very best of health, as it leaves me the same, the photo on the other side is one of the many places in Malta. I will send some more photos later on, of other places. The only thing wrong with Malta is that it's far too warm and the water is very bad to drink. I would give anything for a cool drink of water. Lots of love to you all at home. Sam.

CHP 6 - THE HOME COMING

PORTES-DES-BOMBES, MALTA.

CHP 6 - THE HOME COMING

OS R McCullough Snr with a crew mate from HMS Amethyst.

(Pics courtesy of Raymond McCullough Jnr)

Homeward bound with Malta in the background.

CHP 6 - THE HOME COMING

(Pic courtesy of Glyn Evans – Taken by his father Enoch Evans RAOC at the Suez Canal 1949 as Amethyst made her way back from Hong Kong)

HMS Amethyst approached Plymouth Hoe on November 1st, 1949, with the emotions running through the ship being almost palpable. What seemed to be years in the happening, the crew of HMS Amethyst were almost home. Loved ones and safety was within touching distance but the welcome they received was far from what they expected. Thousands of people had ascended on Plymouth's shores, and they lined the streets to get a glimpse of Amethyst as she neared her berth.

CHP 6 - THE HOME COMING

The roar of the crowd was deafening, and the flash of photographers' cameras lit up the shoreline. 'Pathe News' captured the docking of HMS Amethyst and so began a very different few weeks for the crew. Everyone wanted their interview, reporters jostled with each other to get a firsthand account from any sailor willing to talk. But each sailor knew the implications of jeopardizing the Official Secrets Act and had been well schooled on their journey home as to what they could say. The overall majority told of how they were so glad to be back in Blighty and how they wanted to be home with their families and loved ones.

Some of *Amethyst's* key ratings: fifth from left at back is Stores Petty Officer McCarthy Cook Griffiths is holding his mongrel Peggy, who helped Simon, the ship's cat, to catch rats

Newspaper cutting from Nov 1949 shows HMS Amethyst received a hero's welcome.

(Original pic - Daily Telegraph 1949)

(Pic courtesy of David Bannister)

CHP 6 - THE HOME COMING

Home coming parade, London 1949 - Stoker Bannister circled (Pic - Courtesy of David Bannister)

CHP 6 - THE HOME COMING

The crowds came out to welcome the men of HMS Amethyst, HMS London, HMS Black Swan and HMS Consort home. On a smoggy November day in 1949, not a space was free on the pavements as people wanted to see their heroes of the Yangtze Incident. As they made their way to the Guildhall in London, the Lord Mayor's civic reception awaited them. Their first stop was at St Martin-in-the-Fields for a short thanksgiving service. Tears flowed for Leading Seaman Williams who was there in his specially adapted invalid's Kart, after losing both his legs in the attack on HMS Amethyst. After being cheered on by the crowds again, the parade of heroes made their way to Buckingham Palace to meet and be inspected by King George VI. The civic receptions had begun in Plymouth where every crew member enjoyed being hosted as heroes for a brief period. However, some of the Sailors were now beginning to show the strain of all the attention. Newspapers reported how some of the crews were not enjoying all the fuss and some thought people were going over the top with their hosting. So, once they were all dismissed for home leave, a mass exodus occurred heading towards local trains and for the Northern Ireland boys, another boat journey lay ahead.

M183. Revised October 1939.

Report of Wound or Hurt.

(Name in full)   (Rank or Rating)   (Official Number)

BANNISTER   Sto. Mech.   D/SKX 833916

belonging to His Majesty's Ship Amethyst

sustained the following* wound on April 20th. 1949

*"Injury" or "Wound"

Here describe minutely the nature of the injury sustained as required by Article 1419 of the King's Regulations

A penetrating shrapnel wound of the apex of the Right lung. The shrapnel was removed some days later at the Stevenson Memorial Hospital, Wei Sin.

Personal Description.

Age about 21 years. Born at or near Belfast

Height 5 ft 6 ins. Hair Ginger Eyes Green Complexion Fresh.

Particular Marks or Scars

Linear scar below lower lip. Scar of entry wound of shrapnel below R. Clavicl

Date 18' April Aug. 1949   Signature of Medical Officer

Stoker Bannister headed home with his certificates of wounding.

The Navy, like all the forces, has a strict policy on self-inflicted wounds. So, any wound caused in military life must be certified.

CERTIFICATE FOR WOUNDS AND HURTS

These are to Certify the Right Honourable the Lords Commissioners of the Admiralty that

(Name in full) (Rank or Rating) (Official Number)

BANNISTER S.J.   Sto. Mech   D/SKX 833816

belonging to His Majesty's Ship Amethyst

"Injured" or "Wounded"

was* wounded on April 20th 19 49 as shown on the reverse hereof;

†"Injury" or "Wound."

and that I/we, having enquired into the circumstances in which he received the† wound stated, and having heard the evidence of Sto. Mech. MADDOCKS D/SSX 847014

(Insert Name, and Rank or Rating)

who witnessed the accident, consider that he was then actually On His Majesty's Service in whilst H.M.S.

Here describe the manner in which the injury was received and also the particular act

Amethyst was in action on 20/4/49, he was hit in the Right side of the chest when going to his action station.

CHP 6 - THE HOME COMING

If the Northern Ireland boys thought that the celebrations were over, they were very much mistaken. They boarded the passenger liner, The Duke of Rothesay in Heysham and headed for the Port of Belfast, Northern Ireland. They couldn't have believed the reception awaiting them in Belfast. These men had been talked about for months. Their capture and torment were broadcast over the radio and in all the newspapers. As the passenger liner docked into Belfast the crowd cheered and waved at their returning sons. The local newspaper reported at the time that AS Johnston was the first to become visible to the crowd with the others close behind. Some of the crowd shouted, "We want Sammy, we want Sammy". Stoker Sammy Bannister had a big story to tell and there was no hiding place. Close to his Rainey Street home, bonfires were lit to welcome the boy's home; the biggest bonfire being in Donegal Pass, just off the Ormeau Road. The crowds swayed forward as the sailors disembarked and again the local newspapers, at the time, reported the sailors having to hold onto their caps as the Amethyst cap tallies were highly valuable and sought after. The sailors were all whisked away by their families and a brief spell of respite awaited. However, this was not to last, as their doors were soon knocked with neighbours and reporters all wanting to talk and meet the so-called heroes of the Yangtze River. Stoker Bannister recalled having to sneak out of the back of the house and scurry up the back entries of his Rainey Street home. This was totally unusual for all the sailors and soon, some of them were to meet again in Belfast City Hall. The Lord Mayor of Belfast had arranged a civic reception for the Northern Ireland Boys, and each received a gift from the people of Belfast city.

CHP 6 - THE HOME COMING

After two weeks at home, the Northern Ireland sailors had to
rejoin their Scottish, English, and Welsh crewmates again. Shore
leave was over, and it was back to Navy rules and regulations
for all. Some were very glad to be back on the ocean wave
whilst others struggled. It's normal after a period of home leave
that it takes a serviceman a little while to settle back into
military life. Old friendships and mess deck mates were reunited
but some were drafted to other ships.

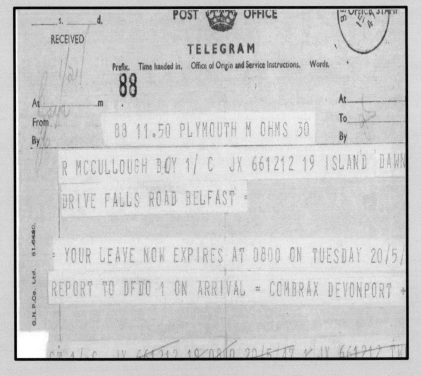

O/Seaman R McCullough's rejoining instructions.

(Pic courtesy of Raymond McCullough Jnr)

CHP 7 – KOREAN EXPLOITS

HMS Amethyst returned to the Far East Fleet and continued in her peacekeeping role. In 1950 she was called into action as a war had broken out between North and South Korea. The war began in June 1950, when North Korea invaded South Korea following heavy clashes between the two. North Korea had strong support from China and the then Soviet Union whilst South Korea was supported by the USA and allied countries. With the South Korean capital, Seoul falling, General Douglas Macarthur stepped in. With the navy cutting off the invading soldiers supply lines, MacArthur's troops drove them back over the 38th Parallel. The whole operation involved over 200 naval vessels and 75,000 troops to recapture Seoul, with the war finally ending in 1953. On board Amethyst was Stoker Sammy Bannister but his friends and crew mates Raymond McCullough Snr and Johnny Murphy had been drafted to HMS Drake. Stoker Bannister had new crew mates to team up with and he became friendly with Petty Officer Denis Augustyn, also a Stoker. They had a particular bond which only came to light later into their Navy life. Augustyn's father had served in the Royal Navy and had been a crew member on board HMS Caroline. Denis' father, Johannes Ludovicus Augustyn was originally from Belgium. He had been involved in the Battle of Jutland and survived to tell the tale. They both weren't to know at the time, but later HMS Caroline was to become a training ship and a member of the Fleet Auxiliary, with her permanent port being Belfast. Stoker Bannister, PO Augustyn and Amethyst survived Korea unscathed, which came to the relief of all on board. They all felt exhausted and had seen enough conflict to last them a lifetime.

CHP 7 – KOREAN EXPLOITS

They had experienced the Second World War as children, some had been in the Yangtze Incident and soon after, Korea. It was time for some much-needed normality.

PO Denis Augustyn of HMS Amethyst.

Denis was the son of Johannes Ludovicus Augustyn

(HMS Caroline)

(Pic courtesy of Ray Augustyn, proud son of PO Denis Augustyn)

CHP 8 - THE YANGTZE INCIDENT FILM

The Belfast Boys, Bannister and McCullough, together with the crew of Amethyst played their part in the daring escape of HMS Amethyst. Slipping out of their captor's hands, from the Yangtze River, July 1949, little did they realize that years later their bravery would be portrayed in a very successful film. Stoker Bannister was contacted by Everest Pictures and his part in the story featured in a large section of the said film. Everest Pictures, London wrote to Sammy Bannister in July of 1956 requesting his permission to allow his portrayal in the film.

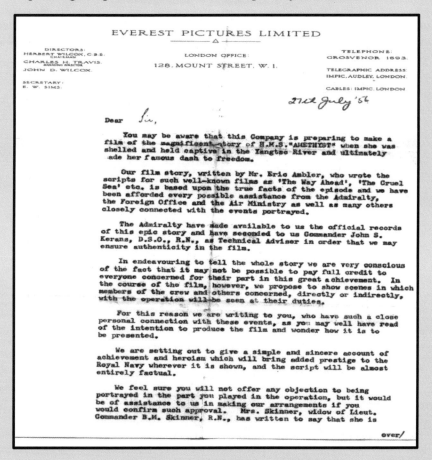

EVEREST PICTURES LIMITED

DIRECTORS:
HERBERT WILCOX, C.B.E.
CHAIRMAN
CHARLES H. TRAVIS.
MANAGING DIRECTOR
JOHN D. WILCOX.

SECRETARY:
E. W. SIMS.

LONDON OFFICE:
128. MOUNT STREET, W. 1.

TELEPHONE:
GROSVENOR 1693.

TELEGRAPHIC ADDRESS
IMPIC. AUDLEY. LONDON.

CABLES: IMPIC. LONDON

27th July '56

Dear Sir,

You may be aware that this Company is preparing to make a film of the magnificent story of H.M.S. "AMETHYST" when she was shelled and held captive in the Yangtse River and ultimately made her famous dash to freedom.

Our film story, written by Mr. Eric Ambler, who wrote the scripts for such well-known films as 'The Way Ahead', 'The Cruel Sea' etc. is based upon the true facts of the episode and we have been afforded every possible assistance from the Admiralty, the Foreign Office and the Air Ministry as well as many others closely connected with the events portrayed.

The Admiralty have made available to us the official records of this epic story and have seconded to us Commander John S. Kerans, D.S.O., R.N., as Technical Adviser in order that we may ensure authenticity in the film.

In endeavouring to tell the whole story we are very conscious of the fact that it may not be possible to pay full credit to everyone concerned for their part in this great achievement. In the course of the film, however, we propose to show scenes in which members of the crew and others concerned, directly or indirectly, with the operation will be seen at their duties.

For this reason we are writing to you, who have such a close personal connection with these events, as you may well have read of the intention to produce the film and wonder how it is to be presented.

We are setting out to give a simple and sincere account of achievement and heroism which will bring added prestige to the Royal Navy wherever it is shown, and the script will be almost entirely factual.

We feel sure you will not offer any objection to being portrayed in the part you played in the operation, but it would be of assistance to us in making our arrangements if you would confirm such approval. Mrs. Skinner, widow of Lieut. Commander B.M. Skinner, R.N., has written to say that she is

over/

- 2 -

most interested and wishes the picture every success.

In view of the co-operation of the Admiralty, the Foreign Office and the Air Ministry, together with the interest and good wishes expressed by Mrs. Skinner, we hope you will see your way clear to confirm your agreement to our portraying you in the film by returning to us the attached Form for which a stamped addressed envelope is enclosed.

If you are in doubt, however, and will kindly communicate with the undersigned, the relevant pages from the proposed film script will be sent you for your approval.

Yours faithfully,
For and on behalf of
EVEREST PICTURES LIMITED.

Stuart Robertson

Stuart Robertson.

Mr. S. J. Bannister,
11, Rainy Street,
BELFAST, N. Ireland.

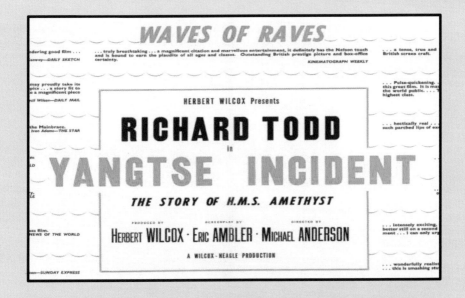

Original Film Poster

Richard Todd and Commander Kerans discussing the forthcoming film.

Dublin born actor Richard Todd (right) portrayed Irish born Commander Kerans' role in the film.

(Pic courtesy of PegasusArchive.org)

Ian Bannen - (Top pic) portrayed Stoker Mechanic Sammy Bannister (Bottom pic)

CHP 8 - THE YANGTZE INCIDENT FILM

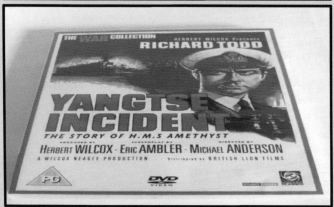

CDR Kerans inspecting the Felixstoe Sea Cadets prior to a screening of the Yangtze Incident.

(Pic courtesy of John Michael Smith - Felixstoe)

Original film posters showing the film to be very popular throughout the world.

CHP 9 - (SM) SAMMY BANNISTER

After the exploits of the Yangtze Incident and the Korean War, Stoker Sammy Bannister continued his service in the Royal Navy until 1953. He then left the Navy with his trio of medals marking the Yangtze and Korean exploits. On Sammy's return to civilian life, he returned to a Belfast where industry was beginning to get back on its feet. He secured employment with Harland and Wolff and settled into a different way of life than what he had experienced in the previous seven years. Belfast was still a tough place to exist in, but the camaraderie and sense of humour was as rife as ever. He was soon to marry his sweetheart, June and settle into married life. In the winter of 1958 along came Sammy and June's first born, Lorraine. Soon to be followed by Grace, David and then Andy (author). So, life was good but tough, and with four mouths to feed, the pressure was on to make ends meet. Being the youngest of four, I wasn't fully aware of most things, never mind the struggles of keeping a family. I was only to learn in later life, the exact way of events. Sammy (my dad) never saw himself as a hero and sometime in the late sixties - early seventies, he went to a local antiques dealer to sell his three medals of service. No one knows exactly how much he received for the said medals, but rest assured it was nothing compared to what they were later to be auctioned for. There was much criticism for my dad to endure for selling his medals but only a parent knows that when it comes to providing for your children, and keeping the wolves from the door, you do what is needed for them, first and foremost. Now that I have medals myself, for serving my country, they don't mean that much to me, the fact that I served is enough.

CHP 9 - (SM) SAMMY BANNISTER

There seems to be a trend nowadays for service personnel to part with their medals, but I think it has more to do with how the government has forgotten about those who have served. Our streets are filled with ex-service personnel who are struggling both mentally and physically. Some in fact are homeless, which is a damming inditement on our government. As myself and my siblings grew up, we became accustomed to watching a so-called war film on TV. This was a special occasion, especially for me, for several reasons. I had heard my older siblings say, "Dad's film is on today" which was a cause for excitement and when something was on TV in those days you had to watch it there and then otherwise you missed it. This was still the black and white stage of television and no video recorders existed either. I was glued to the film every time it was on, anticipating a glimpse of my dad, Stoker Sammy Bannister. The excitement of hearing someone say "Stoker Bannister" on the television and seeing my dad on board a ship was very inspiring for me. Being the youngest sibling, I was not privy to all that was discussed about the part my dad, Stoker Bannister, had in the film but in later years I was to realize this was not just a film. I had always thought my dad, Sammy, had been an actor and had simply been acting in this war film. Once I was shown the scars on his chest and the naval pictures of him in uniform the bigger picture started to unfold. I watched the film with different eyes after this revelation and felt hurt for my dad. The hero status I held for him increased, and I became more inquisitive. He never spoke too much about the Yangtze Incident but would often recall happier times during his time in the Navy.

CHP 9 - (SM) SAMMY BANNISTER

It was either a case of shielding us from the horrors of the incident, his own coping mechanism, or both. His tales of Navy life centered around the camaraderie of his fellow crew mates and their exploits. He would often tell of how the sea would bring even the toughest of men to their knees, praying for it to calm down. I remember, as a young lad, being taken on a sea fishing trip and the sea becoming choppy. I turned to my dad and said, "It's getting rough" to which my dad spent the rest of the day laughing. Dad was invited by a television Company, TSW Television Southwest Limited, to appear in a documentary they were making. He travelled over to England for the 'Distant Guns' Documentary in 1989. It was only when we watched his account on this documentary, that the full explicit horrors of his experience in the Yangtze Incident came to light. My dad never owned a car as we were growing up, so, if it was too far to walk, we got the bus. I remember as a child being taken on the bus from our house to see one of my dad's friends. The bus journey was incredibly long as it was a scheduled service bus, which stopped at every hole in the hedge. Eventually, we arrived in Cookstown, Co Tyrone at the home of Johnny Murphy. My dad and Johnny had kept in touch since the Yangtze Incident, and this was the only time I remember meeting Johnny. He was very welcoming, and his good lady wife, Vera, made us our tea before the long journey home again. Sometime, during my early teenage years my brother and I were looking at my grandfather's medals, who had been killed during the Second World War, it was then I asked my brother, "Has dad not got any medals for what he went through?"

CHP 9 - (SM) SAMMY BANNISTER

At this stage I didn't even know that he had also fought in the Korean War. My brother then told me that dad had sold his medals and not to say anything. As time went on, I was soon to realize that I was one of the reasons for my dad selling his medals, which wasn't a great feeling. I had no idea where they were or how to go about returning them. This yearning to return the medals never left me as I grew from teenager to adult. I began my search at the point closest to home where my dad could have taken his medals, for initial valuation, Smithfield in Belfast. This was possibly the only place my dad could have taken his medals, at this time. As I browsed the numerous medals on display, I soon realized it would be like looking for a needle in a haystack. The shop assistant hadn't even heard of the Yangtze Incident, never mind any subsequent medals awarded. After fruitless browsing and blank looks on the faces of the shopkeepers, it became apparent that they could be out of the country by now. So, as the opportunities arose, through work and travel, I widened my search area too. Unfortunately, as I roamed from antiques dealer to antiques dealer, both at home and on the mainland, I was met with the same reaction or advice, "You will never get those medals back". In England, Scotland, Wales, and Southern Ireland, I was met with shaking heads and despondency. This did not affect my desire or longing to find the medals. I was encouraged by the knowledge that some of the dealers knew what I was enquiring about and could recount the story of HMS Amethyst too. Some dealers were sympathetic whilst others were uninterested.

However, in 1990, when a British computer scientist, Tim Berners- Lee invented the World Wide Web, it brought new hope and access to a wider search net. So, from the comfort of home the trawling and surfing began. Day turned to month and month to year but nonetheless the search was never called off. In between times, unfortunately, my dad Stoker Bannister, in 1996, faced another fight. This time he couldn't see his enemy, but he knew there was something wrong.

Ill health was to visit him again and so began another battle, this time with bowel cancer. During a scheduled operation for the removal of the cancer, his heart stopped. He was shocked a total of eleven times in the space of two days to bring him back. He continued his fight and when questioned during this fight if he was ok, he responded, "yes, but it scares you when you hear the nurses calling you back." He bravely fought against bowel cancer, a damaged heart and failing organs, succumbing to disease on Christmas Eve night,1996. He was only sixty-nine and his passing was devasting for all of us. When we laid him to rest, my determination to repatriate his medals grew to a level which surpassed any previous levels. We were still relatively young in the internet age in 1996 and little did I know what a journey lay ahead for this quest to find my dad's medals. My dad left a lasting legacy in how he brought us up and he also had an effect on his friends and work colleagues. Numerous people with whom my dad worked with were now retired. It became a regular occurrence that they would contact me to inform me that my dad's film was either on, or due to be broadcast.

CHP 9 - (SM) SAMMY BANNISTER

Even they called it, "Your Dad's film" not the 'Yangtze Incident'. 2012 saw my quest to repatriate my dad's medals continue and surfing of the internet intensified. It was then that I came across a trio of medals which looked surprisingly familiar. It was the colours of the ribbons which first attracted my attention and further inspection took place. I then saw the words Stoker and Bannister and I thought I was hallucinating. My dad's medals were staring at me, and I couldn't focus. "Could it be them?" I asked myself, and it was them. His three medals, The Yangtze barred - Naval General Service medal and his two Korean medals. They were being advertised on a dealer's website. I couldn't quite believe it, and I couldn't wait until the next day to contact them. I managed to get through to the dealer the next day, but the news wasn't good. They indeed had been in possession of the medals, but the advertisement was an old one. It became apparent that they used old advertisements like this one for further business and to promote what had been sold before. The medals were gone. Sold in 2008, I was devastated; I had been within touching distance and now was back at square one. However, all hope was not lost. I was actually speaking to a very important person at the dealer's shop. The guy in question had been responsible for overseeing the sale of my dad's medals, so he had some vital information at hand. He was aware of the collector who had purchased my dad's medals together with other valuable paperwork. He was extremely helpful and asked if I wanted him to act as a go-between.

CHP 9 - (SM) SAMMY BANNISTER

He offered to contact the collector but warned me that the said collector lived in the far east, which is quite ironic, given that this is where the medals were won. He warned me it could take a considerable amount of time to contact him. I was delighted and agreed to his help and waited nervously. Day turned to week and week to month and still nothing. Finally, the phone call came; it was a call I had been waiting on for so long yet was dreading at the same time. This time the news was good but came at a price, a hefty price. The dealer had made contact with the collector, and he had eventually come back with his answer. The collector was reluctant to part with the so called 'Jewel in the crown' of his collection, but seeing as I was Stoker Bannister's youngest son, he would agree to sell them back to me.

After I got over the initial shock of this news I waited for the catch, and did it come? The collector was willing to sell the medals and paperwork to me for ten thousand pounds. My heart sank, I felt sick but had to compose myself and try and be rational. This was the news I had been waiting for since I was a boy, now was the time to act. I agreed to the sale and told the dealer I would call the next day to begin proceedings. I had no idea how I was going to come up with the money, but I knew this would probably be my only chance of ever getting the medals back for my dad and the family; so desperate times called for desperate measures. I called the Auction dealer's the next day and left the required deposit, of course the credit card had to be used for this on the pretense of buy now - worry later.

Then I had six weeks to wait and generate the remaining money.
I contacted my good friends at The Somme Centre. The Somme
Centre is a Heritage Centre and educational Museum based in
Newtownards, Co Down, Northern Ireland. It opened in 1994
and promotes the role played in the First World War, by both
Protestant and Catholic soldiers, fighting together. My idea was
that if I could get a grant to purchase the medals, I could then
donate them to the Somme Museum and here they would stay
for future generations to enjoy. Carol and the team at the Somme
Centre couldn't have been more helpful. Almost immediately,
they filled out the forms for a Heritage Lottery Grant and
together we worked on the idea of a 'Yangtze Incident' display
which would be used along with the medals for educational
purposes. Unfortunately, the Heritage Lottery turned us down
and even a second, more detailed application made by the team
was unsuccessful. This was frustrating but not the end of the line
by any means. I wrote and contacted many other agencies and
famous names who came back with the same answer. It became
an answer which saddened me very much and summed up the
apathy shown for the past heroes and fallen servicemen and
women of our countries. The answer was always a resounding,
"Sorry, your story is fantastic, and we wish you every success,
but we cannot assist you with this"; but much like my dad
Stoker Bannister, I never know when I'm beaten, so I struggled
on with my quest. I went to a local newspaper, The Belfast
Telegraph, for help, and they kindly took up my story. Their
reporter, Jamie McDowell contacted me and completed a
fantastic article, which appeared in the said paper.

I want to bring my father's historic medals back home

Andrew Bannister

When his Yangtze Incident war hero father was forced to sell his medals after falling on tough times in the 1960s, Andrew Bannister, a transport planner from Lisburn, finally traced them in Asia, but his quest to get them back was only just starting...

Appeal: Andrew Bannister with a picture of his father Samuel Bannister and his medals

6My father was called Samuel Bannister. He was a stoker mechanic on board the HMS Amethyst. He was working in the engine room of the ship when it was attacked while travelling up the river Yangtze in China during the Chinese Civil War in 1949. It was on its way from Shanghai to Nanking in order to replace the HMS Consort which had been standing guard at the British Embassy in the city when it came under fire from the Chinese Communists — the People's Liberation Army.

The ship was so badly damaged that the crew had to evacuate her. After evacuating and swimming to the banks of the river my injured father and and one of the injured shipmates were taken captive and brought to a vil-

'I'm hoping the public can help get them back'

lage hospital where they were operated on without any anaesthetic. Many others who fled the

would have been in the early days of his marriage and he was finding it financially tough. He decided to sell the medals.

He would have got a fairly good amount of money for them. They were collectors items even then, because a movie called The Yangtze Incident: The Story of HMS Amethyst had come out and raised its profile.

My father passed away in 1996, and since then I've always wanted to have the medals back. Unfortunately, his Yangtze medal is one of the most sought after medals in the world, but my search was made a lot easier by utilising the internet.

after 2006 to a chap who works in the Far East for £6,500.

I knew they were my father's medals because in the photos of on the website they had his ID number and name inscribed along the edge of the Yangtze medal itself.

My heart sank when I heard that they'd been sold, but the English firm agreed to contact the man to see if he would be interested in selling them back to me but the dealer told me not to get my hopes up.

of trying to raise enough funds to retrieve the medals, but as you can imagine, £10,000 is a lot of money. So far I've put a lot of my life savings towards the amount which will reduce it a little.

I recently spoke to the Somme Heritage Centre here to find out if they could offer me any help.

They advised me that a National Lottery grant may be the best way to go about it and they've agreed to support me in my task of getting the medals back

(Original newspaper article - created by Jamie McDowell, Belfast Telegraph)

CHP 9 - (SM) SAMMY BANNISTER

The newspaper article generated some enthusiasm and I have to
say, renewed my faith in the public spirit. Several friends made
small donations and I received a few donations from my dad's
old workmates who were still living at the time. In total I
received one thousand pounds towards my dad's medals and as a
well-known supermarket says, 'every little help's. However, the
pressure was still on, and the Auction Dealers would be calling
soon. So, it was time for action, and some serious thinking. At
the time, I was living very close to my workplace, and I had no
real need for a car so up for sale it went. A week or so later the
car was sold. I was now halfway there with the 10k needed and
still under pressure. The relevant agencies which I had contacted
remained fruitless and time was running out. So, with a very
understanding wife and a bank loan, the full amount was raised.
I waited with trepidation for the Auction Dealer's call and on a
very special day it came. They had received the medals and
paperwork from the Far Eastern Collector and were now ready
to forward them on to me, just as soon as they received my
payment. The transaction was made, and special courier postage
details taken. So, in 2012, my dad's medals were delivered right
to me in my office at work. I can still feel the overwhelming
sense of completion when my dad's medals were in my hands.
I'd done it, my lifetime's dream had come true! Albeit too late
for my dad to see but they were back in the family where they
belonged.

Stoker Bannister's Trio of medals.

So, what next? These medals were meant to be on display – a permanent display, along with the story, for all generations to enjoy. Another quest had begun, one which brought many surprises along the way. I decided that a permanent memorial was needed and not just to my dad but to all his shipmates involved in the Yangtze Incident. I began to research the story even further and I purchased a book by George Hickinbottom, 'The seven Glorious Amethyst's'.

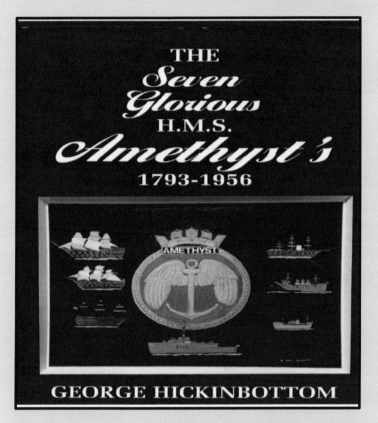

A fantastic book and valuable resource for me in researching my dad's crewmates and the Yangtze Incident story. It was vital in its confirmation of a lot of facts and figures. George also had the idea of medallions being struck for the crew of HMS Amethyst; made from the metal of the ship herself.

The medallions were presented to the crew of HMS Amethyst.

My quest continued and I took my chance when I heard that the Antiques Roadshow was coming to Belfast in 2018. I contacted them and was delighted to receive a response almost immediately. Their presenter, John Foster, came to visit me and hear the story of my dad's medals. He was extremely interested in the story and was able to tell me that they would feature in the show. The show aired in late 2018, and a lot of people contacted me after the show to tell me of their connections to HMS Amethyst and the Yangtze Incident story. They agreed that the story of the Yangtze Incident should be remembered in Northern Ireland as it has been in England, namely at the National Memorial Arboretum. Which is what I hope to achieve soon.

(Pic courtesy of Gail Scragg – daughter of Enoch Evans)

The memorial stone laid in remembrance of all four ships involved in the Yangtze Incident 1949.

The National Memorial Arboretum, Staffordshire England. **(Funded by The Four Ships Association)**

Unfortunately, all the survivors of HMS Amethyst have now passed away but our determination to remember them hasn't. Sammy Bannister died in 1996, but what happened to the others?

Stoker Sammy Bannister.

Raymond McCullough Snr died in 2014.

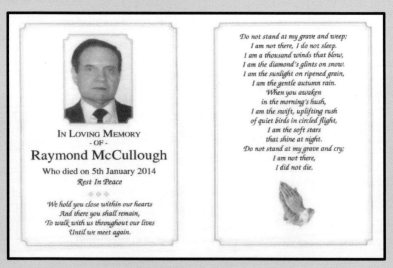

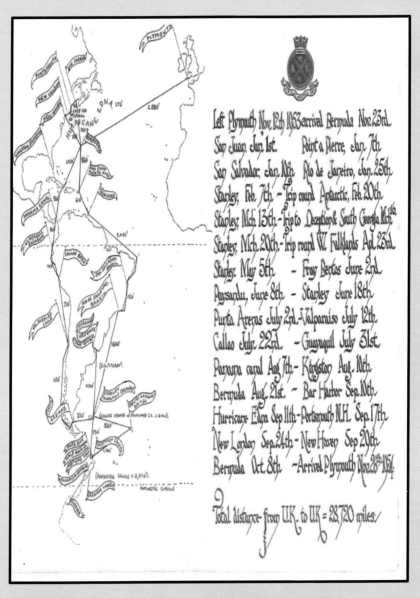

A year in Johnny's life, sailing around South America

CHP 10 - WHERE ARE THEY NOW?

(Pic courtesy of Ciaran Murphy)

Johnny Murphy died in 2016.

After a 30-year career in Post Office Telecoms/BT Johnny attended the 50th anniversary of the Yangtze Incident in 1999. Here he met up with former shipmates. The reunion was organized by the Amethyst Association, a concept of LT Cdr Stewart Hett.

James Foster Johnston

James Foster Johnston died in June 1993 at the age of 65. After leaving the navy he worked for the Coastguard. He served in Kilkeel and Bangor before transferring to Brixham in Devon, England.

CHP 10 - WHERE ARE THEY NOW?

Due to the political situation in Northern Ireland and/or for family reasons, no further details of the remaining sailors from the province are known or wish to be made public - other than the fact they are all now deceased.

Simon the ship's cat.

Simon was also decorated after the Yangtze Incident. He was awarded the Dickin's Medal, the one and only time it was awarded to a cat. Simon unfortunately didn't get to enjoy his shore leave. As the crew of the Amethyst sailed into Plymouth on the November of 1949, Simon had to first go into quarantine. It was here that he fell ill and never recovered. His crewmates gave him a full military funeral and he was laid to rest in at the pet cemetery in Ilford, Essex.

CHP 10 - WHERE ARE THEY NOW?

Kerans John S – Lt Commander (Birr Co Offaly Ireland)
……………....DSO

Commander Kerans made England his home after leaving the Royal Navy and became an MP in 1959. He served in the Conservative Party representing Hartlepool until 1964. He died in September 1985 at the age of 70, so he would have died knowing that the CPLA had admitted they fired first. I'm sure this would have brought some solace to him as he remembered the men lost during the Yangtze Incident.

Kerans John S.

(Pic courtesy of R McCullough Jnr)

CHP 11 – THE GOVERNMENT ENQUIRY

As with most international incidents, it was vital that the government debate was swift to follow the Yangtze Incident. It was well known to the house that the United Kingdom; the Soviet Union and the United States of America had signed the Moscow Declaration in December 1945. Thus agreeing, that they would not get involved in any of China's internal affairs, and they would remain neutral. Prior to the Yangtze Incident, information had been received by way of Military Intelligence, that the Communists were planning on crossing the Yangtze River. However, the intelligence informed that this should be after the 21st of April, giving HMS Amethyst time to relieve HMS Consort at Nanking. Therefore, based on this information, the order was given for HMS Amethyst to proceed. At the government debate, Mr. Churchill asked Mr. Atlee why no one had thought of protecting the Royal Navy ships by means of aerial support, considering that, a not too dissimilar incident had recently taken place in Egypt, but was minimalized by the presence of aircraft support. Mr. Atlee could not respond to this until further investigations were made. Mr. Churchill said there were many unanswered questions, particularly the fact that both the French and USA had withdrawn their ships prior to the Incident but the British had left HMS Consort exposed in Nanking. Mr. Atlee paid tribute to the British forces involved and reported that at present; HMS Amethyst had 27 men wounded and 19 men killed. HMS Consort had 4 men wounded and 10 men killed. HMS Black Swann had 7 wounded and HMS London had 15 men wounded and 13 killed. He then reported that at present 12 ratings were still missing presumed dead.

CHP 11 – THE GOVERNMENT ENQUIRY

The house agreed that HMS Amethyst was lawfully proceeding to Nanking without the need or requirement to have permission or to inform anyone, as foreign ships were, and had been, moving freely in the area prior to the incident. It came to light, during this debate that British consul letters to the communist authorities for the assault on Amethyst to cease, were met with a succinct refusal. The Chinese People's Liberation Army stated that Amethyst had not requested passage and that the British had inflicted heavy casualties on the CPLA. They were, however, willing to allow Amethyst to move on if she helped their troops cross the Yangtze River. This request was blankly refused by the British. The CPLA further alleged that British Forces had entered the Chinese Civil War, by attacking communist forces. Again, this was totally rejected and unfounded. The British Government had not been informed prior to this that their ships would not be furnished with safe and neutral passage along the Yangtze River. The house expressed its sincere thanks to all those involved. The bravery and dedication of the Navy and RAF staff was commended. Special thanks were directed towards the USA, who had remained ready to assist if required. Thanks, was also conveyed to the Chinese Nationalist forces for their support. The house also expressed its sympathy towards the lost and their loved ones. Viscount Swinton addressed the House to seek answers which were blatantly obvious facts - government ministers had failed to act on. He demanded to know why, when the CPLA had advanced so close to the banks of the Yangtze River, and were indeed heavily armed, that no one thought that an imminent crossing and attack was about to take place.

CHP 11 – THE GOVERNMENT ENQUIRY

For him, it was no great surprise that an assault was impending in Nanking. He enquired as to what level of intelligence was passed to ambassadors or naval officers. He found it incredulous that not one official deemed it necessary to approach the Communist Forces to ascertain safe passage and that our ships would not be molested on their journeys. The Viscount also informed the house that he wanted to know, if it was the government's intention to keep the ambassador and his staff so late in the day at Nanking, and why aircraft were not placed on standby to evacuate, rather than leaving our ships exposed. The house unanimously agreed that the overriding question, which required answering, was, when was the intelligence made available and how was it communicated? The House rested and would motion the debate again.

It is unlikely we will ever get the answers to the questions discussed here. However, almost 36 years later, in 1985, the CPLA finally admitted that they fired upon HMS Amethyst first. This does not have any bearing on the military or strategic decisions made by the Royal Navy, they simply followed orders and defended themselves with the utmost bravery.

CHP 11 – THE GOVERNMENT ENQUIRY

Over the years there have been ill feelings from the crew members of HMS Concord (**Not to be confused with HMS Consort**) who met with Amethyst on her escape and were on alert to action stations if required. They were not recognized for their bravery, which is another unanswered question. I have spoken to some of these crew mates and their families over the years and it has always saddened them why they were not decorated along with the other ships.

(Stoker Bannister and two shipmates on board HMS Amethyst, prior to the Yangtze Incident)

HMS Amethyst being scrapped. (Pic courtesy of David Smith)

In 1954, HMS Amethyst started her ramp down. She had seen many skirmishes and although battered, she was repaired and continued her gallant service. Her demise came in the form of joining the Royal Navy's Reserve Fleet. Ironically, she came to Northern Ireland, to the Port at Lisahally, Co Londonderry.

CHP 12 - THE SHIPS

Here, she was to be declassified and made ready for only auxiliary duties. There was much excitement for the employees of Craig's Engineering and Brown's Foundry. They were responsible for the work on Amethyst and the upkeep of the other RFA Vessels. This, of course, was not the end of the story for HMS Amethyst. In 1955 she was made totally seaworthy again for another epic journey. This time, she was to sail onto the silver screen. She was to star in her own film, but tragedy was to visit her for one last time. The Yangtze Incident Film had been commissioned by Everest Pictures and HMS Amethyst was to be the main star. However, she didn't get to make it the whole way through the film. A special effects explosion blew a massive hole in her hull, and she was replaced by HMS Magpie. She was towed for a few shots in the film but unfortunately this is where her life ended. She ended up being scrapped In January 1957, Demmelweek and Redding of Plymouth raised her to the ground, as seen in the previous photo.

CHP 12 - THE SHIPS

HMS London (Pic courtesy of David Smith)

HMS Black Swan (Pic courtesy of David Smith)

HMS Consort (Pic courtesy of David Smith)

HMS Concord (Pic courtesy of David Smith)

Stoker Bannister and a fellow Stoker, sporting their thirty-day beards. A bit of lighthearted relief after the Korean War.

In The Royal Navy, men who wanted to grow beards had thirty days to do so. They would then be inspected by the ship's commander and either passed or declined. This became more stringent from the 1960's onwards. This was because the photographs on their ID cards had to be changed to reflect their new appearance.

AB Johnny Murphy and SM Sammy Bannister's medals re-united 74 years after the Yangtze Incident

In 2023 Ciaran Murphy, proud great nephew of Jonny Murphy came to Northern Ireland for a visit. It was then we were able to take the above photograph. A very special moment for all concerned.

CHP 14 - TWO MORE BOYS FROM BELFAST

When my discovery and retrieval of my dad's medals hit the headlines, it provoked another son of a naval hero into contacting me. Raymond McCullough Jnr knew his naval hero dad had been on the same ship as my dad, so he immediately got in contact. I was amazed and delighted to hear from Raymond and after a very long telephone conversation agreed to meet and exchange stories and photos. Before the meeting occurred, I investigated the ship's crew lists and other information I had and there it was, a group picture of some of HMS Amethyst's crew. Low and behold this picture included Raymond McCullough Snr and my dad, Stoker Sammy Bannister both together on-board Amethyst. Both young men, a world away from Belfast, in the grip of a communist war in China.

(Pic courtesy of G Hickinbottom)

Stoker Sammy Bannister (Left) and Ordinary Seaman Raymond McCullough Snr (Right)

I couldn't wait to meet Raymond and show him this photo and the other information I had. Our initial meeting resulted in a tight bond of friendship which has gone from strength to strength. We both exchanged photos and stories of our fathers and agreed upon our desire to have their epic escape remembered forever. We both made it our pledge that we wouldn't rest until we got a permanent memorial to them and their crew mates from Ireland. We began to research the other crew mates and have since found the grave and memorial stone dedicated to Johnny Murphy in Cookstown.

A lovely tribute to Cookstown's hero Johnny Murphy. Placed as a memorial to Johnny's memory by Cookstown County Council.

CHP 14 - TWO MORE BOYS FROM BELFAST

Raymond McCullough Jnr

As a teenager, Raymond McCullough Jnr learned of his dad's exploits in the Royal Navy. Raymond's dad showed him photos and some items of uniform which had been kept out of sight for many years after his service. Unfortunately, given the political situation in Northern Ireland at this time, making public the fact you had served for the Crown, was something which could bring issues to your door. Which for Raymond Jnr became more and more frustrating as time passed. He could see that his father was proud of the service he had given but had to keep it all under wraps. When Raymond Snr passed away Raymond Jnr was more determined to preserve his father's memory and service. He gathered as much of his dad's naval service memorabilia but could not find his dad's Yangtze service medal. After a few meetings with myself, I made Raymond aware of other medallions his dad was entitled to and through LT Cdr Stewart Hett, Raymond managed to secure these medallions for his late father. Even better news was to come during an intensive search of his mother's house, Raymond found his dad's precious Yangtze medal and rang me to break the fantastic news. Now, both Raymond and my family have our fathers' medals, safe and secure. During many meetings and conversations between myself and Raymond Jnr, I remembered a photograph which was in my mother's photo album. It was a photograph of my late Grandmother (whom I had never met) waiting at Belfast docks for her son to return from the Yangtze Incident.

Alongside her was another woman waiting on her son, this somewhat insignificant photo has now become a revelation, for the other woman in the photo was actually Raymond's Grandmother. This discovery was totally amazing. Once again, I couldn't wait to call Raymond and tell him this news. I can still remember the call to this day. Raymond told me he could not believe it at first. It was like all the pieces of a jigsaw coming together at once. I immediately sent him a screenshot of the said photo.

(Mrs. Dora McCullough and Mrs. Margaret Bannister awaiting their sons' return from the Yangtze Incident, 1ˢᵗ Nov 1949)

These medallions were issued only to the crew of HMS Amethyst in honour of their gallantry and devotion to duty during the Yangtze Incident 1949. They were designed and distributed by former shipmate George Hickinbottom (Mess deck Dodger)

CHP 15 - THE AMETHYST ASSOCIATION

LT Cdr Stewart Hett was the President of The Amethyst Association until he crossed the bar in 2019. Stewart was a young Lt on HMS Amethyst during the Yangtze Incident. He negotiated the release of my dad, Stoker Sammy Bannister, and Boy Seaman Keith Martin. Although I never got to meet Stewart, we had many conversations and discussions by email and telephone. Stewart was a fount of all knowledge regarding the Yangtze Incident. He particularly used this knowledge to help many family members with their enquiries. He answered everyone's queries on the Maritime Quest website Forum. A fantastic website run by Michael W Pocock.

A young Stewart during his Officer Training.

(Pic courtesy of Gilly O'Reilly - proud daughter of Stewart Hett)

CHP 15 - THE AMETHYST ASSOCIATION

I was privileged, along with my siblings, to attend the 2019 Reunion of the Yangtze Incident. Run by the Amethyst Association, it was held in Plymouth, England. Unfortunately, Stewart was unwell, but did manage to pre-record a message to all attending the reunion. Sadly, he crossed the bar a few weeks later and is sadly missed by his entire family circle and friends. He attended the Cenotaph in London for Remembrance Sunday many times, representing the Four Ships Association. He loved to pay tribute to all those who lost their lives during the Yangtze Incident and indeed the two World Wars. Stewart was active in supporting the Sea Cadets and one of his last visits was to the Welwyn Garden City & Hatfield Unit.

Lt. Cdr Stewart Hett MBE RN Retd. Pictured with the Battle Ensign from HMS Amethyst. This was during his last inspection

of the Welwyn & Hatfield Sea Cadets.

(Pic courtesy of Gilly O'Reilly - proud daughter of Stewart Hett)

–

Author with two veterans of the Yangtze Incident. Ray Calcott and Eric Mustoe. Both Ray and Eric served on board HMS Amethyst during the Yangtze Incident. This photo was taken at the 2019 Amethyst Reunion. Unfortunately, both Ray and Eric have since crossed the bar, but it was an honour to meet them both and hear their tales of the Yangtze Incident.

HMS AMETHYST 1949 (Ref- Public Record Office, ADM 16/5704)

Killed - (Surgeon Lt) **JM Alderton**. (CPOSM) OFC **Aubrey**. (SBA) TO **Baker**. (BS) MJE **Barnbrook**. (LSM) W **Barrow**. (OS) CW **Battams**. (SM) L **Crann**. (OS) AE **Driscoll**. (OS) DJ **Griffiths**. (EM) SP **Hicks**. (SM) VD **Maskell**. (SM) DH **Morgan**. (SM) P **Muldoon**. (OS) PJ **Sinnott**. (W) E **Tattersall**. (OS) DG **Thomas**. (AS) AAJ **Vincent**. (OS) RJ **Wright**.

DOW - (OS) GW **Winter**. (Lt Cdr) BM **Skinner**.

Wounded Officers - (Lt) PEC Berger. (Lt) HRM Mirehouse. (Lt) EG Wilkinson.

Severely Wounded Officers - (Lt) GL Weston.

Wounded Petty Officers and Seamen - (SM) T
Anderson. (SM) **SJ Bannister**. (SM) **LGM Canning**. (LS) **AB Crighton**. (AS) **AWJ Davies**. (S) **DC Davis**. (SA) **B Howell**. (SM) **BA Loving**. (SM) **G Maddocks**. (BS) **SR Marsh**. (BS) **KC Martin**. (SM) **FW Morrey**. (PO) **R Nicholls**. (AS) **RC Potter**. (AS) **DR Redman**. (AS) **RG Richards**. (AS) **A Rimmington**. (OS) **B Roberts**. (SIG) **DW Roberts**. (CEA) **ST Roblin**. (SA) **AF Silvey**. (LS) **GL Stevens**. (AS) **MP Tetler**. (SIG) **DH Wharton**.(AS) **EJ Williams**. (OS) **KP Williscroft**.

Severely Wounded Petty Officers and Seamen - (LS)
C Williams. (SM) **R Fletcher**.

HMS CONSORT 8 killed, 2 died of wounds and 20 wounded.

Killed - (PO Telegraphist) **JC Akhurst**. (SM) **RG Gifford**. (CPO) **MJ Gurney**. (AS) **CND Hutton**. (Tel) **E Iredale**. (OS) **S Jenkinson**. (LS) **W Moir**. (PO) **A Morton**. (OS) **CV Theay**. (EM) **J Tobin**.

HMS LONDON 12 killed; 1 died of wounds and 15 wounded.

Killed- (LS) **JH Arkell**. (AS) **AW Ellwood**. (AS) **JP Foley**. (AS) **EGW Harrison**. (Marine) **LH Jarvis**. (OS) **S Jones**. (OS) **JC Lane**. (AS) **WG Pulling**. (PO) **AB Roper**. (AS) **H Shelton**. (CPO) **PJ Stowers**. (OS) **SWA Walsingham**.

(LtCdr) **CR Grice-Hutchinson**. (OS) **GG Warwick**. (Marine) **W Fisher**. All DOW after being hit by gunfire from the shore days after the Incident.

HMS BLACK SWAN 7 wounded.

CHP 17 - WHAT NEXT FOR THE TWO BELFAST BOYS?

Now, Raymond McCullough Jnr and I are pursuing our campaign to have both our fathers and their crewmates recognized. We hope to secure a permanent memorial along the Titanic Quarter for future generations to enjoy. Keeping the Yangtze Incident in people's memories will undoubtedly assist in keeping these brave sailors in remembrance.

(Pic courtesy - Paul McErlane)

Raymond McCullough Jnr and Andy Bannister (Author) - proud sons of two Naval heroes.

CHP 17 - WHAT NEXT FOR THE TWO BELFAST BOYS?

A heartfelt note from Raymond McCullough Jnr.

I believe that my dad and Andy's dad did not receive the recognition they both deserved during their lifetime. I have joined forces with Andy to ensure the recognition and memorial to our fathers and their shipmates becomes a permanent fixture for all generations to enjoy. Their memory and sacrifice will not go untold for any longer. This book and our joint venture will ensure that. Only for the bravery of the five ships involved in the Yangtze Incident, Andy and I would not be here today to tell their story. My uncle Derek is the last remaining sibling of my dad's family and has been truly inspirational in providing more information about my dad's young life. After my dad died in 2014 a representative of the Amethyst Association informed me about Andy and how his father had been on HMS Amethyst. He told me of a newspaper article Andy had been in, regarding his dad's medals. I looked up this article and Andy had included an email address which I used to try and contact him. I was delighted when Andy responded to my email, and we have been as close as brothers ever since. We had countless meetings and exchanged photos and stories, the most fascinating is the photo Andy had of our two grandmothers. We managed to have a brief display of our fathers' memorabilia and a model of HMS Amethyst which I made. This brief display took place in the Pump House adjacent to HMS Caroline in Belfast.

CHP 17 - WHAT NEXT FOR THE TWO BELFAST BOYS?

A heartfelt note from Raymond McCullough Jnr, continued.

HMS Caroline is now a floating museum run by the NMRN. It is here that Andy and I are hoping that we can secure a permanent memorial to all those sailors involved in the Yangtze Incident 1949. My friendship with Andy and our investigations have resulted in a greater understanding of the trauma and suffering our fathers endured during the Yangtze Incident. This has answered a few questions I always had regarding my dad and how he handled this trauma, both at the time and after he left the Navy. My dad worked for The General Post Office, which later became British Telecom, as a technician, later moving into a management role. My dad would take me fishing in Adrglass, Co Down at the weekends and we would visit my cousins there too. I knew my dad loved the sea and Ardglass, but it wasn't until later in life that I realized why. As I got into my late teens the situation in Northern Ireland was very tense between the two communities. I remember my dad being very uptight about this and warning me never to tell anyone he had been in the Royal Navy. I couldn't fully understand why, but of course, I was to learn later the implications of this news being made public. Looking back, it must have been so frustrating for him, knowing he went through hell on the Yangtze and then could never talk about it. He was obviously suffering and at the same time trying to lead a normal life. Much like Andy's dad, his family came first, and his own issues and suffering were put to the back of his mind.

A heartfelt note from Raymond McCullough Jnr, continued.

Dad was a very religious man and always ensured we attended Chapel, and of course, our shoes were polished, and we were immaculately dressed. His Royal Navy standard of dress and presentation never left him, and he wouldn't tolerate being late either. I remember having to write an essay at school about anyone in the family who had served in the war. I wanted to write about my dad, but my mum reminded me of the dangers of this, so I wrote about my late grandfather who had served in the First World War. This was a safer option for the family and would ensure my dad wasn't exposed as a British sailor. During my dad's final days, I found him on one occasion, lying under his bed shaking and crying. I got my sister to immediately phone for an ambulance. I gave my dad my word that I wouldn't let him be taken away as he was terrified of not coming home again and he knew he was surely in his final days. After this, I stayed with my dad, both day and night, and watched him relive the trauma he had suffered over the years due to the Yangtze Incident. My dad would tell me to stand back as he was hosing the area and other things I couldn't understand. Only now can I see that he was reliving the experiences of being on board HMS Amethyst during the Yangtze Incident. My dad was not easy to live with over the years. Only in his last few years did he open up and tell me of what he had suffered. He told me how it was so difficult because he had to hold everything in that he had come through, not being able to openly discuss it and, like most of that generation, he was too proud to ask for help.

CHP 17 - WHAT NEXT FOR THE TWO BELFAST BOYS?

A heartfelt note from Raymond McCullough Jnr, continued.

I'm sure Andy's dad experienced much of the same as well as bearing his physical scars. Only Andy and I seem to realize and appreciate what our dads went through and as we hold onto our precious memories of them, we are their voice and will fight constantly until we achieve our aim of having them recognized. This is the only way I can explain how I feel about this, and I know Andy probably understands me more than most would.

The more I think about growing up, experiencing my dad's mood changes, the more respect I have for him and his shipmates for how they got on with their lives and bringing up children even though they were still suffering from PTSD. I personally feel that I couldn't have dealt with it. Respect to my dad Raymond McCullough Snr and his shipmate Stoker Sammy Bannister, two boys from Belfast and survivors of the Yangtze Incident 1949.

I will continue with Andy to ensure we achieve our aim of a permanent memorial to our dads and their shipmates.

God bless them all.

CHP 18 - THE BELFAST BOYS AND THE YANGTZE INCIDENT

Three bells (3 o'clock on board HMS Amethyst 1950)

(Pics now in the public domain)

(The beating heart of HMS Amethyst 1950)

CHP 18 - THE BELFAST BOYS AND THE YANGTZE INCIDENT

FURTHER READING

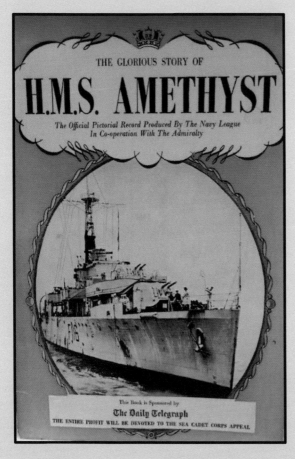

A very rare book, mostly found on eBay. Some great pictures can be found in this 1949 edition.

FURTHER READING

A fantastic insight into Naval terminology- I think this should be issued to all recruits six months before they enlist.

EG: the **(Andrew)** a well-known nickname for the Royal Navy- especially when referring to your length of time in the Senior Service - 'Fifteen years in the Andrew and most of that time spent at sea'. Possibly due to the fame of Lt Andrew Miller, an 18th Century Press Gang Officer.

EG: **(Anchor Faced)** A term of endearment for someone, usually an officer, who lives and breathes the navy, even when retired.

FURTHER READING

A great read by the late George Hickinbottom.

FURTHER READING

Some believe this to be the best adaptation of the Yangtze Incident story.

CHP 18 - THE BELFAST BOYS AND THE YANGTZE INCIDENT

ABBREVIATIONS

AB- Able Seaman

OS- Ordinary Seaman

LH- Leading Hand

PO- Petty Officer

CPO- Chief Petty Officer

C IN C- Commander in Chief

CPOSM- Chief Petty Officer Stoker Mechanic

LSM- Leading Stoker Mechanic

SPO- Stores Petty Officer

RFA- Royal Fleet Auxiliary

Lt-Lieutenant

Lt-Cdr-Lieutenant Commander

Capt- Captain

NA- Nationalist Army

Col- Colonel

CPLA- Chinese People's Liberation Army

Flt Lt- Flight Lieutenant

RN- Royal Navy

RAF- Royal Air Force

KIA- Killed in Action

HMS- His Majesty's Ship (Pre 1952, when Queen Elizabeth was coronated and all RN ships became Her Majesty's Ships)

MID- Mentioned in Dispatches

RAOC- Royal Army Ordinance Corp

DSO- Distinguished Service Order

Jnr- Junior

Snr- Senior

ADMTY- Admiralty

SM- Stoker Mechanic

Retd- Retired

CHP 18 - THE BELFAST BOYS AND THE YANGTZE INCIDENT

ABBREVIATIONS

CWWG- Commonwealth War Graves

FES- Far East Station

BBC- British Broadcasting Corporation

HM- His/her Majesty

NMRN- National Museum of the Royal Navy

ID- Identity

MBE- Member of the British Empire

MP-Member of Parliament

EM- Electrician's Mate

W- Writer

SBA- Sick Berth Attendant

DOW- Died of Wounds

SA- Stores Assistant.

S- Seaman

BS- Boy Seaman

SIG- Signalman

CEA- Chief Engine room Artificer

EA- Engine room Artificer

Crossed The Bar- Died

Tel- Telegraphist

PTSD- Post Traumatic Stress Disorder

DOW- Died of wounds.

Amethyst wounded, who were flown home, were there for the reunion. L./S. Cyril Williams, who lost both legs, and S./M. R. Fletcher, on crutches, both went aboard.

Murphy, McCullough, and Bannister.

Happy Homecoming Smiles at Larne yesterday morning when the Mayor (Alderman Clem Robinson) greeted Petty Officer John M'Carthy, of H.M.S.

John McCarthy receives a hero's welcome in his native Larne 1949.

ULSTER WELCOMES AMETHYST HEROES—The High Sheriff with Stoker-mechanic S. J. Bannister, of Rainey Street, and his fiancee (right). On left is Able Seaman John Murphy, of Cookstown, and Mrs. R. J. R. Harcourt at the civic reception given in the City Hall, Belfast, to local men who served in the memorable action.

FIRST MAN OFF

First Amethyst man off the Duke of Rothesay was Able Seaman James F. Johnston, Bangor, who was accompanied by his father. He was met by his mother and Councillor James Halley.

He was taken by car to Bangor Town Hall, where he was welcomed by the Deputy Mayor (Alderman F. Logan), Alderman Lieut.-Colonel H. T. Porter, M.C., and Mr. R. M. Moore (Town Clerk), and entertained to tea.

Standing, unobtrusively, inside the shed was Able Seaman Frederick Burns, of the frigate Black Swan, which had unsuccessfully attempted to free the Amethyst.

A.B. Burns, who resides at Joseph Street, Belfast, had joined up with A.B. Johnston and A.B. Haveron.

They were members of the first frigate flotilla at Hong Kong and when Johnston and Haveron were posted to the Amethyst it was their first break. He had last seen his pals in Hong Kong.

TOOK CARE OF HIS HAT.

One by one they left, but there was no sign of Stoker-Mechanic Samuel J. Bannister.

"We want Sammy, we want Sammy," chanted the crowd.

Stoker Bannister appeared at last with his mother—smiling cheerfully in contrast to the last time I interviewed her when her son was in a Chinese Communist hospital.

One of the first to greet Stoker Bannister was his girl friend, Miss Lillian Gourlay. She took his much-sought-after hat and he was steered through the crowd.

He did not get very far for he was

THE BELFAST BOYS AND THE YANGTZE INCIDENT

SPECIAL THANKS.

In chronological order.

Raymond Augustyn… For your support, contributions, and pictures.

David Bannister… For your support, contributions, advice, and pictures.

Jennifer Bannister…Proof reading.

Bronwen Dark…Professional Proof reading.

Glyn Evans… For your support and pictures.

Mick Higginbottom…For your support and pictures.

Derek McCullough …For your information and support.

Raymond McCullough (Jnr) For your support, contributions, and pictures.

Paul McErlane… For your support, contributions, and pictures.

Gail Scragg… For your support and pictures.

David Smith…. For your picture contributions.

Jim Waddell…Artist (Cover painting of HMS Amethyst)

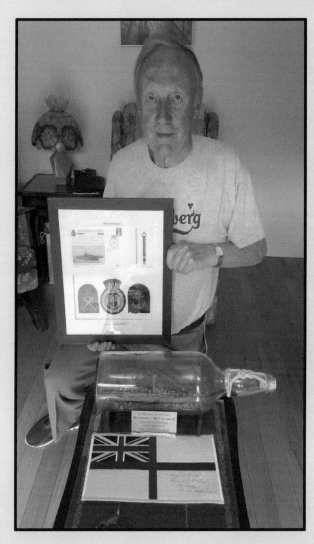

Derek McCullough. Pictured with his brother's memorabilia from HMS Amethyst. Derek is the last remaining sibling of OS Raymond McCullough Snr.

(Pic courtesy of Raymond McCullough Jnr)

Thank you for purchasing this book. I hope you enjoyed it and will keep an eye out for the permanent memorial dedication. The proceeds of this book will go towards the cost and upkeep of the memorial, so on behalf of the Belfast Boys and their crewmates from Ireland, splice the mainbrace.

(Pic on license from PONY5)

(NORTHERN IRELAND BOYS) L-R

McLean, Bannister, Murphy, McCullough, White, and Haveron.

Thank you for purchasing,
'The Belfast Boys and The
Yangtze Incident'.

Andy Bannister.

Printed in Great Britain
by Amazon

25956293R00089